"Sympathy and Solidarity"
and Other Essays

D1564260

feminist constructions

Series Editors: Hilde Lindemann Nelson and Sara Ruddick

Feminist Constructions publishes accessible books that send feminist ethics in promising new directions. Feminist ethics has excelled at critique, identifying masculinist bias in social practice and in the moral theory that is used to justify that practice. The series continues the work of critique, but its emphasis falls on construction. Moving beyond critique, the series aims to build a positive body of theory that extends feminist moral understandings.

Feminists Doing Ethics
    edited by Peggy DesAutels and Joanne Waugh

Gender Struggles: Practical Approaches to Contemporary Feminism
    edited by Constance L. Mui and Julien S. Murphy

"Sympathy and Solidarity" and Other Essays
    by Sandra Lee Bartky

Forthcoming books in the series by

Bat-Ami Bar On, Anita Allen, Amy Baehr, Nancy Potter, Joan Mason-Grant, Eva Kittay and Ellen K. Feder, Margaret Urban Walker, and Chris Cuomo

"Sympathy and Solidarity" and Other Essays

Sandra Lee Bartky

ROWMAN & LITTLEFIELD PUBLISHERS, INC.
Lanham • Boulder • New York • Oxford

ROWMAN & LITTLEFIELD PUBLISHERS, INC.

Published in the United States of America
by Rowman & Littlefield Publishers, Inc.
4720 Boston Way, Lanham, Maryland 20706
www.rowmanlittlefield.com

12 Hid's Copse Road
Cumnor Hill, Oxford OX2 9JJ, England

British Library Cataloguing in Publication Information Available

Library of Congress Cataloging-in-Publication Data

Bartky, Sandra Lee.
  "Sympathy and solidarity" and other essays / Sandra Lee Bartky.
    p. cm.—(Feminist constructions)
  Includes bibliographical references and index.
  ISBN 0-8476-9778-9 (alk. paper)—ISBN 0-8476-9779-7 (pbk. : alk. paper)
  1. Feminist theory. 2. Sex role. I. Title. II. Series.

HQ1190 .B383 2002
305.42'01—dc21   2001048800

Printed in the United States of America

♾™ The paper used in this publication meets the minimum requirements of
American National Standard for Information Sciences—Permanence of Paper for
Printed Library Materials, ANSI/NISO Z39.48-1992.

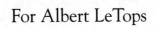

For Albert LeTops

Contents

Acknowledgments

The essays in this collection have taken shape over a long period of time. Many people have contributed to my work, and I wish to thank all of them for their generosity and investment of time. I hope I have not forgotten anyone; if I have, I apologize. I have read most of these papers at a number of conferences and professional meetings. On all of these occasions, the critical response of my audiences helped me develop my ideas. I owe very special thanks to Isaac Balbus, Michael Stocker, David Kim, Judith Gardiner, Charles Mills, Iris Marion Young, Alison Jaggar, Linda Nicholson, Elaine Miller, Ladelle McWhorter, Claudia Card, Margaret Urban Walker, Neal Grossman, Margaret McLaren, Diana Tietjens Meyers, Margaret Morganroth Gullette, Samuel Fleischacker, Yolanda Estes, Bat-Ami Bar On, Lisa Tessman, Ann Ferguson, Bob Stone, Betsey Bowman, Dion Farquhar, Lorraine Code, David Schweickart, Paul Gomberg, and Nancy Frankenberry.

I owe special debt to the academic editors of this series: Hilde Lindemann Nelson and Sara Ruddick. "Sally" Ruddick, in particular, went over these essays with the finest of fine-toothed combs, objecting here, calling for clarification there, often challenging quite central points. If this collection has merit, it is owed in no small part to her careful and critical readings. I also wish to thank Eve DeVaro of Rowman & Littlefield for her patience and forbearance.

The project as a whole would not have been completed were it not for the fellowship I was awarded by the Institute for the Humanities of our College of Liberal Arts and Sciences. The burdensome business of writing philosophy was much lightened by the utopian environment of the institute, the intellectual and moral support of the other fellows, and the warmth and encouragement I received throughout this most special year from its director, Mary Beth Rose, and from the assistant to the director, Linda Vavra.

Finally, I wish to express my profound gratitude to my life's companion, Algirdas Vileisis, for the patience and loving support he has provided me for what is now almost half my life.

Parts of this book have appeared in the following earlier versions.

Chapter 2, "Agency: What's the Problem?" from *Provoking Agents: Gender and Agency in Theory and Practice*, edited by Judith Kegan Gardiner (Urbana: University of Illinois Press, 1995). Copyright © 1995 by the University of Illinois Press. Reprinted by permission.

Chapter 3, "'Catch Me if You Can': Foucault on the Repressive Hypothesis," from *Calvin O. Schrag and the Task of Philosophy after Postmodernity*, edited by Martin Beck Matuštík and William L. McBride (Evanston, Ill.: Northwestern University Press, 2002). Copyright © 2002 by Northwestern University Press. Published 2002. All rights reserved. Reprinted by permission.

Chapter 4, "Sympathy and Solidarity," from *Feminists Rethink the Self*, edited by Diana Tietjens Meyers (Boulder, Colo.: Westview Press, 1997). Copyright © 1997 by Westview Press, Inc. Reprinted by permission of Westview Press, a member of Perseus Books, L.L.C.

Chapter 6, "Phenomenology of a Hyphenated Consciousness," originally titled "Story of a Hyphenated Consciousness," from *Marginal Groups and Mainstream American Culture*, edited by Yolanda Estes et al. (Lawrence: University Press of Kansas, 2000). Copyright © 2000 by the University Press of Kansas. Reprinted by permission.

Chapter 7, "In Defense of Guilt," from *On Feminist Ethics and Politics*, edited by Claudia Card (Lawrence: University Press of Kansas, 1999). Copyright © 1999 by the University Press of Kansas. Reprinted by permission.

Introduction

The leitmotifs that connect the essays in this collection are twofold: first they bear some relationship to feminist topics and themes in philosophy or else to my own evolution as a feminist thinker; second, most deal with the social reality of oppression especially in the disguised and extremely subtle ways it can be manifested. Initially, I thought that nothing linked these essays, focused as they are on a variety of thinkers and topics. But then I looked more closely.

"Oppression" is a complex concept, for it can take a variety of forms. Iris Young lists five "faces" or modes of oppression: exploitation, marginalization, powerlessness, cultural imperialism, and violence[1] What these "faces" of oppression share, I venture, is this: they prohibit or make it excessively difficult for persons to exercise the sorts of functions we believe are constitutive of personhood; these prohibitions are unjust and they are a consequence of the actions of other persons, the oppressors. Oppression can be subtle, as in the sort of stigmatizing behavior that can go on behind the backs of both the one who is stigmatized and the one who is doing the stigmatizing, i.e., it can occur beneath the level of conscious awareness; or it can be genocidal, as in the various holocausts of history.

I realize that this talk of "personhood" will send shivers down the spines of those readers who are sympathetic to poststructuralism; they may even send this book crashing against the wall in fury, as I did with—well no matter. But I do not believe that we can have a feminist politics without some conception of what is good for women and what is not, and this, in turn,

1

implies a larger conception of what is good for persons generally and what is not. I recognize fully the danger that first-world feminists, coming out of a national background of exploitation and imperialism, will impose alien and entirely self-interested norms on disadvantaged women; for this reason, I think that our best move is to encourage the development of a truly global feminism, a development that is already under way. In this way, women in societies unlike our own can work out their own analysis and strategies for liberation. We must not overestimate our influence elsewhere: women in other societies are fully capable of taking from first-world feminism what they find useful and scuttling the rest. At any rate, I do not see how we can regard ourselves as feminists and still not condemn what is currently being done to women in Afghanistan or the use of rape as an instrument of mass terror as in Bosnia. Child prostitutes as young as nine fetch up to 60,000 rupees, or U.S. $1,250 at auctions where Arabs from the Persian Gulf bid against Indian men who believe that sleeping with a virgin cures gonorrhea and syphilis.[2]

To talk of "personhood" or of women's subjectivity is not, as some have claimed, a way that feminist theorists, especially feminist academics can aggrandize themselves by putting their own experience at the center, hence marginalizing women not sufficiently privileged to be able to theorize their own oppression. This talk of "self-aggrandizement" seems ironic to me, given the extent to which feminist philosophy is still marginal in many ways and many places. Nor is talk of "personhood" or "subjectivity" a reference to some timeless essence, thought quite rightly to be a dubious move since women who don't fit the definition are ignored, or else their experience of life is distorted.

Normative notions of personhood or subjectivity are *essentially contested concepts*. We argue incessantly about what they mean, since their meaning is tied to our political goals and not all feminists share a single vision. This incessant contestation is, on the one hand, the sign of a healthy movement; but lately it seems that feminist theorists are obsessed with the question whether there are really "women" (or just "differences") in ways that threaten to become irrelevant to any practical political goal.[3] This debate about "essentialism," and the meaning of the word "women," reminds me of debates that raged among American Jews when I was a young teenager. The establishment of the State of Israel caused an identity crisis in American Jewry. What, if any, were our obligations toward the new state? Were we obligated to emigrate and build a new society? Could one be a Jew and not a Zionist? For that matter, could one be a Jew and an atheist? No consensus was reached on these and many other related questions; nevertheless there were still Jews.

These debates call to mind the seemingly endless discussions in postmodern feminism of whether feminism has a "subject"; differently put, whether one can speak of "women" in very general ways. These questions have had the salutary effect of forcing first-world feminist theorists to deal with their own ethnocentrism and in the case of white feminists, their unintended racism.

The effort to find a synthesis of Marxism and feminism, as well as the critique of traditional Marxism, nourished my feminist philosophical imagination for many years. At some point, this effort seemed played out, though I still believe that feminists ignore the rich theorizing around issues of class at their peril. The phenomenon of globalization will require theorists to look carefully at the nature and effects of capitalism in its current stage and whether it affects men and women differently. The powerful cultural critique produced by Second Wave feminism, especially the critique of "femininity," nourished me philosophically too as I struggled to express (and sometimes to transform) this critique into an idiom that would interest a varied readership. I find myself at the end of this road, as well. While I take much postmodern feminism seriously, I cannot see myself being drawn into what appears to be its central problematic, to wit, endless and sometimes agonizing controversies where feminist thinkers try to salvage some concept of feminist politics from conceptual systems (e.g., Lacanian psychoanalysis) that are relativist and determinist. I find that I can stay connected to feminist philosophy only if I continue to explore what it was that drew me to it in the first place—oppression, my own and that of other women, especially internalized oppression, which often appears in highly disguised fashion. Hence, several of the essays in this collection testify to my encounter with poststructuralism; many do not deal directly with feminism, though all are animated by a desire that springs from feminism—the desire to understand the modes and mechanisms of oppression. The last two chapters deal with racial oppression—not from the point of view of the oppressed, but from that of the oppressors. There are also chapters that deal with "ageism" and "anti-Semitism."

The first essay in the collection, "Suffering to Be Beautiful," is a link between my older and newer interests. It is directly a sequel to a much anthologized paper on the female body from an earlier collection, entitled "Foucault, Femininity and the Modernization of Patriarchal Power."[4] In fact, whole chunks of that paper reappear in this one, simply because I couldn't think of any better way to say what I had already said. However, the current version responds to some criticisms of the earlier version. I still maintain that "disciplinary practices," as such practices are understood by Foucault in *Discipline and Punish*, are importantly involved in the process whereby a female body is turned into a "properly" feminine one, nor have I retreated from the position that this process is, on the whole, disempowering to women. I have tried to construct a more systematic enumeration of just what this disempowerment entails, also a systematic list of the ways in which we are coerced, bribed, and even blackmailed into going along with it. I try too to develop two themes that are surely underdeveloped in the earlier paper. First, pleasure. I try to respond to the criticism that I have undertheorized the pleasure we take in turning ourselves into properly feminine women[5] by spelling out in more detail the nature of these pleasures.[6]

The second theme I neglected in earlier treatments of the topic is ambivalence. It is very likely impossible for any woman raised conventionally, as I was, to write without emotion or without ambivalence on these matters. It may be the case that the business of trying to achieve, as near as one can, physical perfection, is even more burdensome than my treatment of the topic suggests, or else there is far more pleasure at stake here than I am willing to admit to myself and to my readers. This the reader must decide. I think that there is considerable psychic ambivalence at work here, a phenomenon that is echoed, I hope, in my treatment of the ambiguity of meaning carried by the various disciplinary practices themselves. As students of philosophy, we learned that "everything is what it is and not some other thing." But in the present case, this is false: the disciplines of the body are in and of themselves complex: for example, the memory of acquiring and exercising them may be tied to a powerful nostalgia for the past, for one's youth, for friends who have somehow drifted away.

The next three chapters relate directly to the poststructuralist turn in feminist theory, namely, the question of the status of the subject, in particular, the strife between "essentialist" theories of the subject and those that foreground "difference." Having devoted a good deal of attention to female subjectivity and female sexuality, I found it necessary to open myself to criticism implied by much poststructuralism, namely that I had conceptualized "the subject" in ways that were fundamentally flawed.

Now there is really no such thing as "poststructuralism," i.e., there is no "ism." There is instead congeries of theories, some having virtually nothing in common, others sharing some "family resemblances." As it was impossible to focus on every thinker on whom this title has at some time rested, I decided to focus on a thinker widely held to represent this tendency: Michel Foucault. Foucault's texts are relatively lucid and many of his ideas have been incorporated into contemporary feminist theory.[7] I myself had written a successful paper drawing heavily both on Foucault's analysis of disciplinary practices directed toward the body that have shaped the modern subject, also his claim that domination changes its character in the transition from feudalism to modernity.

Now Foucault is widely thought, at least in his major works, to have announced the "death of the subject," the view that we are wholly constructed within socially dominant discourses and practices, that we are "effects" of "regimes" of power and knowledge and that therefore we lack the self-determination that has been thought traditionally to characterize the moral agent. But if moral agency is an illusion, so is political agency: where then does this leave feminism, or any other movement for social reconstruction?

In "Agency: What's the Problem," following Peter Dews's exposition of Foucault's ideas in Discipline and Punish and The History of Sexuality, Vol. 1, I argue that Foucault implicitly assumes what he explicitly denies, i.e., some measure of self-determination on the part of the subject.[8] Hence, Foucault does not nullify the subject; he presents an incoherent, i.e., an inconsistent theory of agency, but an incoherent theory of agency is no theory at all. In the later volumes of the History of Sexuality, Foucault shows us (male) agents in antiquity who are quite a bit freer than his modern subjects: they seek and sometimes achieve balance, moderation, and self-determination in the design of their sexuality. Since the late Foucault puts forward a conventional notion of agency, and the earlier Foucault an incoherent, hence self-nullifying theory of agency, agency is safe, at least for now from at least this poststructuralist. I close the chapter with an attempt to diagnose the inconsistencies in Foucault's treatment of the sexual subject: these I trace to a conception of power that is so expansive it leads inevitably to confusion.

I am aware that my slash-and-burn critique of Foucault in "'Catch Me if You Can': Foucault on the Repressive Hypothesis" will irritate and even anger many who find Foucault's analyses in Volume 1 of the History of Sexuality to be among the most illuminating in contemporary philosophy. But my critique of his critique has been sticking in my craw since 1980, when I first encountered it. Over the years, I found more and more that feminist theorists tend to accept Foucault's understanding of the subject, of sexuality, of knowledge and power as if these views were self-evident. Whenever I face an oppositional consensus, I assume that I am in the wrong. I think that is why it took me so long to write this chapter. I argue that most of the reasons Foucault offers to reject concepts of repression developed, e.g., by left-wing followers of Freud, are by no means persuasive. I argue too that the paradigmatic case Foucault offers as an illustration of what goes on in "repressive" situations has a game-like, playful quality; the effects of repression, I suggest, are painful and destructive. Wherever the truth lies, it seems clear to me that Foucault's account of repression seriously neglects the sense of guilt, the dysfunction, the shame, and the general misery that have to be told as part of this story. Moreover, I argue that Foucault seriously misrepresents the views of his antagonists, whom I take to be Freud and the Freudo-Marxists, nor can an account of anything like sexual repression afford, as does Foucault's, to neglect unconscious processes.

"Sympathy and Solidarity" was likewise inspired by poststructuralist concerns. It has long been charged that feminist theory has taken the experience of privileged white women in current or formerly imperialist states to be essential, and the experience of all other women to be marginal; this has come to be called the "problem of difference," the problem being the "occlusion" of differences among women. Various diagnoses are offered by contemporary poststructuralists, most of whom indict the entire Western tradition in philosophy, for example, for "logocentrism," the mistaken belief that there is some ultimate unitary word, presence, essence, reality, or truth that can provide a foundation for theory, experience, and expression. While I deal more fully with these theories in the body of the chapter, suffice it to say here that the problem of difference has been conceived in largely cognitive terms, i.e., as allegiance to a flawed theory of meaning or an untenable metaphysics.

I treat the problem of difference not as fundamentally a metaphysical or an epistemological problem, but as a political issue.[9] The problem, it seems to me, has to do with the building of solidarities among women who differ markedly from one another in terms of privilege—of race, nationality, sexual orientation, etc. Now the best builder of solidarities is joint work, but in joint work there is still the problem of understanding the Other and her view of the world in her difference from myself. I resuscitate, for the purposes of the essay, Max Scheler's phenomenology of *Mitgefühl*, literally "feeling-with" or perhaps "sympathy."[10] I find in this canonical figure resources for conceptualizing both barren as well as more fruitful access to the disadvantaged Other. I find too that Scheler's account is sketchy and needs to be supplemented. This chapter was, for me, a voyage of discovery into a phenomenological universe I had never entered. The chapter is dense and layered: all sorts of directions for further inquiry suddenly reveal themselves, as well as questions, especially about the widespread *absence* of sympathy, the excessive privatization that characterizes contemporary life in societies like ours. I take this to be a political as well as a moral problem.

In "Unplanned Obsolescence: Some Reflections on Aging" I treat aging as more or less of a calamity, focusing not on the physical disabilities that many aging people must face, but on the loneliness that often accompanies the loss of friends and perhaps an intimate Other, and on the growing obsolescence of one's moral, cultural, and intellectual perspective. While the analysis is not formally gender-specific, I note the particular disabilities aging women face as a consequence of the cultural figurations of femininity. I study the strategies that some older women have adopted to counter their social depreciation. Mindful of criticisms of my work that I do nothing but diagnose social evils and never offer strategies of resistance, I end the chapter by outlining a number of strategies that are worth considering. I conclude by imagining a strategy for women only, which will irritate and perhaps shock some readers, though I hope that others will try it.

"Phenomenology of a Hyphenated Consciousness" was written for an anthology on marginalization. I first thought of writing on women as a marginalized group, which I think we largely are, but everything I imagined saying seemed stale and repetitious. Then I remembered typical introductory sociology texts in which Jews are normally taken to be paradigmatic of a marginalized people—"marginalization" in this case, referring to those who live partly in and partly outside, i.e., on the margins of the dominant political, economic, social, and cultural "center." Here was my subject: I was, after all, a Jew and so I had a fund of personal experience on which to draw. The essay itself is largely autobiographical, showing how at least one person, myself, navigated an initially depreciated social identity. I close by looking briefly at patterns of other Jewish-American identity formations without comparison or judgment. I uncover at the end, something I had not gone looking for (these works often take on a life of their own, as characters in novels are said to do!), namely a host of questions about the particular duties and responsibilities of persons who affirm an ethnic identity.

Like the chapter on the repressive hypothesis, "In Defense of Guilt" had been sticking in my craw for many years. The persons who initiated me into radical politics had utter contempt for "liberals," especially for "guilty liberals," indeed, the ideas of "guilty" and "liberals" were virtually impossible to pry apart. But so powerful was *that* consensus that I was rendered speechless. This made me profoundly uneasy, as I had been a "liberal" for many years prior to my radicalization, and because I knew that deep down, I felt guilty because of advantages I enjoyed that were systematically denied to many other people. In this chapter, I argue that "guilt," understood as a recognition of one's complicity in injustice, is an acceptable motive for political action (philosophy paper as act of revenge!). I maintain that white persons are complicit (whether they want to be or even recognize that they are) in the functioning of a racial caste system that bestows upon them (typically at the expense of others) unearned privilege.[11] I sketch a number of white-skin privileges to make vivid how privilege is embedded for whites *in what we do not see and never experience*. I distinguish guilt as complicity from other forms of guilt and speculate concerning ways of lessening the complicity of whites in an unjust racial hierarchy.

"Race, Complicity, and Culpable Ignorance" is the last chapter in the collection; in it, I extend and expand one of the principal themes of "In Defense of Guilt," namely, the cognitive and affective strategies used by whites to allow themselves to live in a state of denial concerning their own complicity in the perpetuation of racism. My approach is phenomenological, though I touch upon at least one psychoanalytic theory of racism. The "subject" in this chapter is a "nice" white person, someone who says he abhors racism, admires Dr. Martin Luther King Jr., and is shocked and outraged by the Aryan Nation and the Ku Klux Klan.

These final essays on racism are my first efforts at writing anything publishable on this topic. I find this much more difficult than writing about sexism; the difference lies of course in my own relationship to the two forms of oppression. There are dangers that lie in wait in both cases. When I write about sexism, I am writing from the perspective of the victim; but when I write about racism, I write from the social location of the victimizer, the oppressor. In condemning "nice" white people I am condemning myself. I am a white person, indeed, a "nice" white person. I am, to some degree or another, revealing myself in ways that make me squirm. One of my editors chided me for writing about "nice" white people with contempt and even hatred. The contempt and shame we feel for our own people is often more intense than what we feel for the Other. I have since modified my language, recognizing that racism in white people is far more than a moral flaw, including as it does, the "common sense," what Heidegger would have called the "average everydayness" for whites of racist attitudes.[12] It is difficult for most people to leave the herd consciousness of the herd. I know these people; they are my family; they were our neighbors in the suburbs; some of them are people I love. But proper academic writing—so far—has been allowed only a posture of detachment and "objectivity." Writing about racism generates in me complex and intense feelings that are not normally expressible within the proper parameters of proper philosophical writing. Such writing is always expected to "keep its cool," which is only another way of pointing to its androcentricity. The writing style in which we learn to do philosophy reflects the traditional subject of much modern philosophy, namely, the Cartesian cogito.

In the case of sexism, there is of course the danger of overgeneralization, hence ethnocentrism and unintended racism, discussed earlier. There is also the danger that here, as in the case of racism, one's anger and outrage will escape the restrictions put upon one's self by the stylistics of academic prose and overflow the essay. The tears must be wiped off the page before it goes to the printer. But what is the matter with allowing anger and outrage to inflect one's writing? The taboo on the expression of emotion in philosophical writing reflects the no longer universally held belief that reason and emotion are distinct and that if one expresses emotion, one's text will be lacking in rationality, objectivity, and proper detachment.

Another danger is that one's work may well be taken as an exaggerated and somewhat superannuated lament lacking relevance for women today ("Well, maybe it was that way for *your* generation . . ."). Even if one's work is taken seriously by those readers for whom it is principally intended, there is still a good number of mainstream philosophers for whom feminist philosophy has no authentic philosophic content, so is nothing but a lament after all. And this judgment gave rise, for some in my generation of feminist philosophers, to a kind of self-doubt that I hope will die out with my generation, the advance-guard of the Second Wave. Younger feminist philosophers ought to be able to go about their business free of such self-doubt. But secretly, some of us worried some of the time that our critics might be right after all, that what we were doing wasn't *really* philosophy. In fact, we were struggling to expand the scope of "real" philosophy in ways that were then and are still quite radical. So we stuck it out.

The personal voice—my voice—is prominent in many (but not all) of these chapters. I have only just learned that an important trend currently in literature is the writing of memoirs by "ordinary" people. "Important" people—statesmen, diplomats, generals—have always written their memoirs, but what is happening now is the writing of memoirs by private people, those who lack celebrity status and whose names are not household words. Sometimes these writers of memoirs have some small distinction, sometimes not.

Now the use of the memoir and of the personal voice has entered philosophy by way of feminism.[13] The fact that I have allowed my own experience and my own memories to be expressed in some of these chapters is perhaps a revolt against the impersonal and detached style of the Cartesian subject, though while I was writing these essays, I had no conscious intention to start a revolt. Thinking it over, I see that it is a pretty good idea, when coupled (of course) with careful analytic distinctions and persuasive argumentation.

Part of the reason, I think, for the tremendous success several years ago of the Feminist Ethics and Social Theory Conference in Clearwater, Florida (out of which, quite spontaneously, the group FEAST was born), was due to the presence in many papers of the author's voice. This gave to the scholarship presented there a vibrancy and immediacy that is normally lacking in philosophical writing. The feminist critique of the abstract subject of traditional philosophy, whose "view from nowhere" allows him (*sic*) no determination by

race, class, gender, age, ethnicity, or sexual orientation, is now finding expression, I think, in the style in which the new philosophy is being done.
There is no reason to think that a philosopher's experience of life or her memories, expressed directly, cannot buttress an argument or broaden the conceptual scope of a subject area; indeed, the inclusion of the personal voice can
make a philosopher's moral or political vision more vivid and more compelling. So, I do not appear before my readers, particular persons that you are,
disguised as a Mind Thinking, but as the particular person that I am. The
voice in these chapters is my own.

Notes

1. Iris Young, *Justice and the Politics of Difference* (Princeton, N.J.: Princeton University Press, 1990), 39–69.

2. Robert I. Friedman, "India's Shame: sexual slavery and political corruption are
leading to an AIDS catastrophe," *The Nation*, April 8, 1996, pp. 11–20. "There are lots of
rich men in India who can afford to buy virgins so they won't get AIDS," says Maureen
Aung-Thwin, a Human Rights Watch official. "Men brag about it" (p. 12).

3. "Feminist politics, up till now, appears to be grounded in a modernist category,
'woman,' with essentialist implications, while the possibility of founding a political program on a postmodernist base is, to say the least, still a matter for debate." Margaret Whit-
ford, Introduction to *The Irigiray Reader* (Oxford: Blackwell, 1991), 13.

4. Sandra Bartky, *Femininity and Domination: Studies in the Phenomenology of Oppression* (New York: Routledge, 1990).

5. Oral communication from Dion Farquhar, University of California at Santa Cruz.

6. However I did approach the subject earlier from the standpoint of narcissism and I
was quite clear as to the nature and extent of the narcissistic pleasures that can arise in
the course of satisfying the demands of what I call in that chapter "the fashion-beauty
complex." Perhaps the treatment there was still too negative. See "Narcissism, Femininity and Alienation," in Bartky, *Femininity and Domination*.

7. See especially Judith Butler, *Gender Trouble* (New York: Routledge, 1990).

8. Peter Dews, *Logics of Disintegration* (London: Verso, 1987).

9. Of course, political positions have normally tacit epistemological and metaphysical underpinnings. The question has to do with the best access to the problem. My approach resembles what old-time radicals would have called the "theory of the party."

10. Following Scheler, I avoid the term "empathy." This point becomes clear in the
body of the chapter.

11. See Charles Mills, *The Racial Contract* (Ithaca, N.Y.: Cornell University Press,
1997).

12. It was Iris Young who first pointed out to me the similarities between racist attitudes as "common sense" and the Heideggerian notion of "das Man," translated as "the
one." Example: my mother told me once: "One doesn't wear white shoes after Labor Day."

So who exactly is "the one"? It is everyone and no one in particular. Ideas float about for which no one takes responsibility. I lived in a racially mixed neighborhood for ten years; at family parties, my relatives would ask, disapprovingly, "Aren't there lots of *them* down there?" They drew on what they assumed was the shared understanding of "the one." "One simply wouldn't live in high-crime areas." "Their neighborhoods are dirty, etc." None of this was spelled out, for we both knew that it was implicit in the first question.

Heidegger's idea of an anonymous everyday understanding is echoed in Sartre's conception of bad faith and Nietzsche's contempt for "the herd."

13. While not standard practice, this idea is hardly new. The late William Earle thought that most philosophy was and should be acknowledged as "existential autobiography."

CHAPTER ONE

~

Suffering to Be Beautiful

I. Introduction

Some months ago I had coffee with a female student who was enrolled in a course I was teaching called "Sex Roles: Moral and Political Issues." The student, a self-identified feminist, liked the course. She praised the way I handled controversy in the class. She was impressed with my grasp of the subject and with my success in getting students to take seriously ideas they found not just unfamiliar, but often threatening or even offensive. Naturally, I ate all of this up. Who wouldn't? Then my student ventured what sounded like consummate praise: "And you do all this," she said, "without sacrificing your femininity." I was filled with dismay. Carol, my student, was not familiar with my work (I rarely teach it) and she had no way of knowing that I had been writing polemics attacking femininity for at least a decade. Not wanting to appear churlish, I muttered something about femininity's being a very complex notion and just let it go.

Thinking about this later, I realized that Carol was, in a way, right about me. My teaching style is generally warm and nurturant, just what students expect from a female teacher. I avoid the pedagogy of sarcasm or confrontation as much out of cowardice as conviction. I might describe my style too as "seductive," i.e., I try to charm students into liking me so they'll like the course, hence take seriously my invitation both to learn something new and in the course of this learning, to subject received opinion to critical scrutiny. A brilliant female scholar I know who teaches in the Ivy League and who was perhaps the youngest woman ever to be appointed to a full professorship in her institution, told me that she couldn't help but relate to her classes as if they were parties at which she was the hostess and the students her guests, just as if they were tea parties and not seminars. She said she found this feeling of constraint in herself quite burdensome. Of course I saw myself in her and we had a good laugh at each other's expense. And then I thought about what I wore to school. I'm not up there in fatigues and combat boots. Now that nice silk blouses can be had for under thirty dollars, I often wear those and I often wear skirts. I like jewelry, not flashy or expensive jewelry, just "nice" jewelry. I care about what goes with what; I accessorize; my friends say I look "put together." I'm always flattered when someone tells me I look "put together."

So why am I writing polemics against femininity, yet comporting myself in ways that fall more into the "feminine" than the "masculine" slot? Now, on the face of it, my little inconsistencies or even my vanities, are hardly of general interest. But is there perhaps an interesting theoretical problem lurking here somewhere? The feminist critique of many aspects of "normative femininity" is one of the glories of Second Wave feminist theory and I am happy to have made some small contribution to it. The question that may well be lurking behind the contradictions in my own life is this: have feminist theorists produced a theory (here a critique of normative femininity) for which (for reasons not yet articulated) there is no effective practice? And how useful is theory without practice? Political theory should be nourished by political practice; it should guide practice but, in turn, it should be modified if effective practice so requires.

II. Suffering to Be Beautiful

My topic is not the female, but the feminine body and the feminist critique of the cultural norms that teach us what it is to achieve and to maintain such a body. Femininity: what is it and what's wrong with it? The *Oxford English Dictionary* defines "femininity" as "the quality or assemblage of qualities pertaining to the female sex." (982). The dictionary is mistaken. One can be a member of the female sex and yet fail or refuse to be feminine; conversely, one may be a biological male and a drag queen. "One is not born a woman, but, rather becomes one" (Beauvoir 1974, 301); what de Beauvoir has in mind is the "properly" feminine woman. Femininity is a set of qualities of character and behavioral dispositions as well as a compelling aesthetic of embodiment.[1] The two cannot be entirely disentangled. What, traditionally, have been thought to be the character traits and behavioral dispositions of the "truly" feminine woman?

Such a woman, I venture, is warm, nurturant, expressive, unaggressive, gentle, and genteel, in ways that persons of the upper class are thought to be genteel: she would not, for example, scream obscenities at someone who cut her off on the highway. The stereotypically feminine woman, like God in some medieval theologies, is defined more in terms of what she isn't than what she is: what she isn't, i.e., what she lacks is what is traditionally regarded as the stereotypically masculine. So the properly feminine woman, unlike the properly masculine man, isn't ambitious on her own behalf though she may be ambitious on behalf of her husband and children. She isn't possessed of physical courage: at least, she isn't disgraced if she exhibits cowardice in the presence of physical danger, even in the presence of a mouse. This woman may be competent in the kitchen or in her boudoir, but she may not exhibit too much competence in those domains we regard as "masculine"—which include domains in which power is typically exercised. While this is changing rapidly, the woman who exhibits too much competence in current or formerly male spheres of activity may well put her femininity in danger. If she doesn't, this is noteworthy, hence my student's compliment: I was competent and *nevertheless* feminine. The truly feminine woman is not independent as we expect men to be independent: she is not disgraced if she solicits and accepts all sorts of help from other people, including financial support from a man. If she is out driving and lost, she suffers no loss of face in stopping at the nearest gas station to find out where she is. The truly feminine woman has peculiar skills in the domain of human relations. She creates around herself an atmosphere of serenity and acceptance; skilled in the management of conflict, she sees to it that everyone is properly served at the tea party of life. Finally (and I do not claim that my list is complete), the properly feminine woman, if she is young enough, is sexually appealing, this is because not only her soul but her body too exhibits the proper marks of normative femininity: it is, in the words of Judith Butler, "a mode of enacting and re-enacting received gender norms which surface as so many styles of the flesh" (Butler 1985, 11).

There is a question, first of all, what it is to inhabit a feminine body, in particular, a body that exhibits the "styles of the flesh" that now hold sway. Phenomenological philosophy has tried to rehabilitate embodied experience in spite of its almost total neglect in the work of its founder, Edmund Husserl. However, to the degree that phenomenologies of embodiment have taken male embodiment covertly as emblematic of embodiment per se, they have merely recapitulated the male bias that marks the Western philosophical tradition as a whole. This can be remedied by setting aside "normal" phenomenology, i.e., the search for the a priori, necessary structures of any embodied consciousness whatsoever in favor of an analysis of the structures of meaning embedded in the experience of an historically, culturally, and sexually specific subject. Without saying explicitly that she is doing so, Simone de Beauvoir practices such "situated" phenomenology in *The Second Sex*.

Iris Young's classic "Throwing Like a Girl: A Phenomenology of Feminine Body Comportment, Motility and Spatiality" finds that a space seems to surround women in imagination: this manifests itself both in a reluctance to reach, stretch, and extend the body to meet resistances of matter in motion—as in sports or in the performance of certain physical tasks—and in a typically constricted posture and general style of movement. A woman's space is not a field in which her bodily intentionality can be freely realized but an enclosure in which she feels herself positioned and by which she is confined (Young 1989). Re-reading this earlier work, Young has herself found that the piece takes as paradigmatic the white, middle-class experience. Be this as it may, the piece has value not only in that it does indeed describe the spatiality and comportment of many women but because it lays out the norms of properly feminine motility, norms that, unsurprisingly, reflect values of the dominant social groups, whether they elicit conformity or not.

The properly feminine body exhibits a specific repertoire of gesture, posture, and movement. This body must learn to display its charms, but discreetly. The properly feminine woman must never allow herself to sprawl into the available space. She must avoid the looseness in body comportment which is the mark of the "loose" woman. Fashion magazines, from time to time, offer quite precise instructions on the proper way of getting in and out of compact cars: these instructions combine the three imperatives of woman's movement: discreet body display, restricted spatiality, and grace. These instructions warn a woman not to allow her arms and legs to flail about in all directions. She must try to manage her movements with grace—no small accomplishment when one is climbing out of the back seat of a two-door Honda Civic. At least in the West, a woman must learn to be guided physically by a man in a way that normally goes unnoticed. Males in couples may literally steer a woman everywhere she goes: down the street, into elevators, through doorways, around the dance floor. The man's movement "is not necessarily heavy and pushy or physical in an ugly way; it is light and gentle but firm in the way of the most confident equestrians with the best trained horses" (Henley 1977, 149). In regard to its size and its various parts, the properly feminine body must remain within the appropriate parameters and it must display itself, again within the proper parameters, as an ornamented surface.

I shall argue in what follows that the imposition of normative femininity upon the female body requires training, that the modes of training are cultural phenomena properly described as "disciplinary practices," and that the discipline they represent is disempowering to the woman so disciplined. I follow Michel Foucault in defining discipline as a "system of micropower that is essentially non-egalitarian and asymmetrical" (Foucault 1979, 222). Disciplines of the body in general fragment and partition the body's time, its space, and its movements; in this case, they drill the recruit to the disciplinary regime of femininity in the proper techniques necessary to maintain the current norms of feminine embodiment. Later, I shall examine as well the profound ambiguity that femininity has for women: its seductiveness as well as the pain it causes and its hold on our very identities.

Consider, for example, dieting as a disciplinary practice of femininity. The current body of fashion is taut, small-breasted, and narrow-hipped; its slimness borders on emaciation; it is a silhouette that seems more like that of an adolescent boy or a newly pubescent girl than a mature woman. It seems that the more women appear in what was formerly masculine public space, the less space our bodies are to occupy. Since most women do not look like adolescent boys, they must diet. National studies have shown that the majority of American women are on a diet *all the time*. Girls as young as nine and ten are now beginning to diet (as many as 40 percent, according to the National Heart, Lung, and Blood Institute, cited in *USA Today*, August 12, 1996). Virtually every major women's magazine has a dieting or exercise regimen (or both) in every issue. Women greatly outnumber men in self-help groups such as Weight Watchers and Overeaters Anonymous—in the case of the latter, by well over 90 percent (Millman 1980). Fat can now be eliminated surgically, by liposuction; women, not surprisingly, avail themselves of liposuction in far greater numbers than men. While women typically perceive their bodies as too large, sometimes, as in the case of breasts, they are seen as not large enough; hence the frequency of surgical breast augmentation, and its side- and after-effects have since become a national scandal.

Dieting disciplines the body's hungers: appetite must be monitored at all times and governed by an iron will. Since the innocent need of the organism for food will not be forgone, one's body becomes the enemy, an alien being bent on thwarting the disciplinary project. Anorexia nervosa and bulimia, now approaching epidemic proportions, are to the women of today what hysteria was to women in the nineteenth century: "the crystallization in a pathological mode of a widespread cultural obsession" (Bordo 1985). Women who fall into the dreaded category of "overweight" are often seen as morally deficient individuals who lack self-discipline and suffer from weakness of will.

What is regarded as the inability to control one's appetite for food has taken on the moral stigma formerly reserved for those who could not control their appetite for sex: the "overeater" as libertine, unable to resist the "sinfully delicious" (Bordo 1995). Columnists for upscale magazines like *Vogue* find, not only in the "overweight" but in all those who refuse the disciplinary program, no moral deficit, rather a mild psychological disturbance. Women who refuse to shave their legs or to get regular manicures are exhibiting a deficiency of self-esteem, which accounts for their refusal to care properly for their bodies.

Exercise is of course a part of this disciplinary regime. There are modes of exercise meant for women only, these designed not to firm or to reduce the body's size overall but to resculpture its various parts. M. J. Saffon, "international beauty expert," assures us that his twelve basic facial exercises can erase frown lines, smooth the forehead, raise hollow cheeks, banish crow's feet and tighten the muscles under the chin" (Saffon 1981). Not just her body but the very expressions of her face can subvert the disciplinary project of bodily perfection. As an expressive face lines and creases more readily than an inexpressive one, if women are unable to suppress strong emotions, they can at least learn to inhibit the tendency of the face to register them. Sophia Loren recommends that a piece of tape be applied to the forehead or between the brows that will tug at the skin when a woman frowns and remind her to relax the face. Loren recommends that the tape be worn whenever a woman is home alone (Loren 1984).

I turn now to another category of disciplinary practices: skin care. A woman's skin must be soft, supple, hairless, and smooth; ideally, it should betray no sign of wear, experience, age, or deep thought. Hair must be removed not only from the face—with tweezers, hot wax, foul-smelling depilatories—or, for a more permanent result, by painful and expensive electrolysis[2]—but from large surfaces of the body as well, from legs and now, with the new high-leg and thong bathing suits and leotards, from much of the pubic area. The development of what one "beauty expert" calls "good skin-care habits" requires not only attention to health, the avoidance of strong facial expressions, and the performance of facial exercises, but the regular use of skin-care preparations, many to be applied oftener than once a day: cleansing lotions (ordinary soap and water "upsets the skin's acid and alkaline balance"), wash off cleansers (milder than cleansing lotions), astringents, toners, make-up removers, night creams, day creams, nourishing creams, eye creams, moisturizers, skin balancers, body lotions, hand creams, lip pomades, suntan lotions, sun screens, and facial masks. Black women may wish to use "fade creams" to "even skin tone." Skin-care preparations are never just sloshed onto the skin but applied according to precise rules: eye cream is dabbed on gently in movements toward, never away from the nose; cleansing cream is applied in outward directions only, straight across the forehead, the upper lip, and the chin, never up but straight down the nose and up and out on the cheeks. If this regimen, dermabrasion, and chemical peeling fail to disguise the effects of aging, as sooner or later they must, there is always the scalpel, i.e., the face lift.

The ordinary circumstances of life as well as a wide variety of activities cause a crisis in skin care and require a stepping up of the regimen as well as an additional laying on of preparations. Skin-care discipline requires a specialized knowledge: a woman must know what to apply if she has been skiing, taking medication, doing vigorous exercise, boating, swimming in chlorinated pools; if she has been exposed to pollution, heated rooms, cold, sun, harsh weather, the pressurized cabins on airplanes, saunas or steam rooms, fatigue or stress. Like a schoolchild or prisoner, the woman mastering good skin-care habits is put on a timetable: Georgette Klinger requires that a shorter or longer period of attention be paid to the complexion *at least four times a day* (Klinger and Rowes 1978).

I offer dieting and skin care merely as examples of the disciplinary practices of femininity; the whole story would take too long to tell, and so I pass over in silence such things as manicure, pedicure, hair care, and punishing aerobic exercise. The language of "beauty experts" recognizes quite explicitly the disciplinary character of their project ("There are no ugly women," said Helena Rubinstein, "only lazy ones"). Women's fashion magazines try to disguise the disciplinary character of their body regimens.[3] For example, the application of cosmetics is often presented as an aesthetic activity in which a woman can express her individuality. I would dispute this. While cosmetic styles change every decade or so and while some variation in makeup is permitted depending on the occasion, making up the face is, in fact, a highly stylized activity that gives little rein to self-expression. Painting the face is not like painting a picture: at best, it is more like painting the same picture over and over again with minor variations. Little latitude is permitted in what is considered appropriate for the office and for most social occasions; indeed, the woman who uses cosmetics in a genuinely novel way is liable to be seen not as an artist but as an eccentric. Furthermore, since a properly made-up face is, if not a card of entree, at least a badge of acceptability in most social and professional contexts, the woman who chooses not to wear cosmetics at all faces sanctions of a sort that will never be applied to someone who chooses not to paint a watercolor.

Now the imposition of discipline is not always disempowering. One thinks, for example, of the discipline involved in mastering Zen meditation.

Arguably, the discipline I had imposed upon me and that I imposed upon myself in graduate school was empowering: my degree allowed me (entering the academic job market at a propitious time) to find challenging and, in time, secure employment at a decent wage (indeed, at a wage far above what most women in the workforce earn). But I will argue that, on balance, the disciplinary practices that produce normative embodied femininity are indeed disempowering to women.

Item: The disciplines of femininity are an enormous drain on women's time and women's money. I assume that women could put their time to better use (vocational training, perhaps, or political agitation!). In a world so marked by misery and hunger, the billions spent on cosmetics could be put to far better use.

Item: Women submit to this discipline in large measure because we have been persuaded that our faces and bodies are defective. A variety of cultural discourses and practices have brought it about that we inhabit what I have called elsewhere an "inferiorized" body (Bartky 1990). "Inferiorization" has both objective and subjective moments. The objective moment has complex determinants, but represents, at the most obvious level, the happy marriage of patriarchy to profit. A "fashion beauty complex," as much an articulation of patriarchal capitalism as the "military-industrial complex," presides over the forms in which the sexual objectification and self-objectification of women will manifest themselves. Overtly, the fashion-beauty complex glorifies the female body; more important is its covert aim, which is to depreciate this body. A host of discourses and social practices construct the female body as a flawed body that needs to be made over, hence the popularity in magazines and TV of the "makeover." The media images of perfect female beauty that bombard us daily leave no doubt in the minds of most women that we fail to measure up; we submit to these disciplines against the background of a pervasive sense of bodily deficiency, perhaps even of shame. It is, I venture, the very pervasiveness of this sense of bodily deficiency—like the pervasiveness of a sense of sin—that accounts for women's widespread obsession with the body and the often ritualistic character of our daily compliance. ("I can't go out without putting on my face.")

Item: The disciplines of femininity feed racism and class oppression. The beauty ideal toward which beauty discipline is directed is still largely white and northern European in character; ideal beauty is normally the beauty of the women of those social groups in the "developed" world that have social, economic, and cultural primacy. Hence the popularity of hair-straighteners and "fade-creams" among African-American women, eye-slant removing operations for Asian women, and "nose-jobs," now a virtual rite of passage for many adolescent Jewish girls. The market for blue contact lenses is growing in Bangkok, Nairobi, and Mexico City. Many poor women lack the time and resources to provide themselves with even the minimum of what such a regimen requires, e.g., a decent diet or membership in a health club. Here is an additional source of shame for poor women who must bear what our society regards as the more general shame of poverty.

Item: Alienation. To live in an inferiorized body is to be alienated from one's body, hence from oneself. I am defective not just for others but for myself: I inhabit this body; yet I live at a distance from it as its judge, its monitor, its commandant. I speak of fragmentation: a typically male connoisseur, formed complexly by a host of discourses, resides within the consciousness of most women. We stand perpetually before his gaze, subject to his evaluation. There is some truth to the claim that "women dress for other women." Who but someone engaged in a project similar to my own can appreciate the *panache* with which I bring it off? Insofar as women live within the constraints of compulsory heterosexuality, we know for whom this game is played: we know that a pretty young woman is likelier than a plain one to become a flight attendant or to get the requisite amount of attention in the singles' bar. This interiorized witness which is, after all, *myself*, has put me under surveillance. It is disempowering to be perpetually under surveillance, as even the British royal family has discovered.

Item: The witnesses for whom the feminine body is constructed as spectacle are external as well as internal: we are under surveillance from without as well as from within. Hence, competition among the judged for the judges' approbation; hence the beauty contest, the street hassling, hence the male students on my campus who lounge on benches in the spring and call out to passing women, with appropriate catcalls and sounds meant to suggest kissing: "Hey, baby, you're a nine" or, very loudly, "Hey, get a load of this one, not even a two." The sense of entitlement that allows these young men to set themselves up—successfully, to judge by the embarrassment of women who must run this gauntlet—is simply a local expression of the male entitlement they enjoy generally. It is our superiors who judge us; indeed, the power to judge is part of what it is to occupy a superior position in the first place.

Item: Consider now what meanings are inscribed in the ideally feminine body. Women's typical restraint in posture and movement are understood to be a language of subordination when they are enacted by men in male status hierarchies (Henley 1977). The current ideal body type lacks flesh and substance; it takes up little space. Is this perhaps a response to anxiety generated by the increasing visibility of women in public space (Chernin 1981)? This is also a body in whose very contours the image of immaturity has been inscribed. The requirement of a smooth and hairless skin underscores the theme of inexperience: an infantilized face must accompany this infantilized body, a face that never ages or furrows its brow in thought. I harbor the suspicion that this infantilized body mirrors what one might call, with only a little exaggeration, the effort at a continuing social infantilization of women.

Item: The disciplinary project of femininity is a setup: it requires such radical and extensive measures of bodily transformation that virtually every woman who gives herself to it is destined to fail. Diets are notorious failures: normal aging processes cannot be disguised forever; the face-lift, painful and expensive, must be regularly repeated. Since every woman is under a virtual obligation "to make the most of what she has," failure may become still another occasion for shame.

Item: Consider finally the situation of those women who, through luck as well as assiduous attention to proper discipline, have become famous beauties. To succeed in the provision of a beautiful or sexy body gains a woman attention, admiration, even money, but little real respect and rarely any social power. Further, this envied status must contend with an entire cultural tradition that has traditionally elevated mind over body, spirit over flesh, hence masculinity over femininity. Even women admired most for their bodily beauty complain routinely of their situation in ways that reveal an implicit understanding that there is something demeaning in the kind of attention they receive. Marilyn Monroe and Elizabeth Taylor wanted passionately to become accomplished actresses, that is to say, *artists* and not just "sex objects."

I do not think that the critique I have offered concerns matters which are trivial, though this is how it will appear to many; certainly, there are matters more pressing than the question whether or not we should choose to follow Georgette Klinger's regimen for baby-soft skin. At stake here is what Judith Butler has called the "performance" of gender, indeed the performance which *is* gender and the skills and techniques that are required by a successful performance (Butler 1990). The idea of the feminine comes more and more to be identified with women's sexuality and appearance, and less, as in the past, with women's maternity. As some of us come more and more to escape the domination of fathers, husbands, and clergymen, the norms of ideal feminine appearance and the disciplines we impose on ourselves come to represent submission to new forms of domination. Furthermore, the requirement that we "look like women" is perhaps the most visible way in which we are marked by gender. This compulsive and compulsory marking serves the identificatory purposes of a system of caste privilege. Marilyn Frye expresses this nicely: "Constant sex-identification both defines and maintains the caste boundary without which there could not be a dominance-subordination structure" (Frye 1983, 33). "Elaborate, systematic, ubiquitous and redundant marking of a distinction between two sexes of humans is customary and obligatory . . . the phenomenon is absolutely pervasive and deeply entrenched in all the patterns of behavior which are habitual, customary, acceptable, tolerable and intelligible" (21). But our story is only halfway told.

III. Siren Songs of the Feminine

An obvious question now presents itself: if the culture of beauty is as oppressive as my analysis would suggest, why is it that so many women appear to have capitulated to it? Indeed why do so many women appear to embrace it with enthusiasm? The production of femininity is more perplexing and multivalent than the analysis so far has shown. The ethico-political phenomenology of feminine embodiment in the venues I have been examining is tangled and ambivalent. I offer next a catalogue of what it is that holds us so tightly in the grip of a set of oppressive cultural norms.

First, the obvious; it is hard to get and then to keep a job, even a poorly paying job, unless one presents oneself as a woman who has submitted in some degree, to the disciplinary practices of femininity. Some firms, e.g., law firms and brokerage firms, enforce a very rigid dress and appearance code: here is discipline if ever there was discipline. Not only jobs are on the line: unless she belongs to a radical political subculture (and these have mostly vanished) a woman who has (arguably) the misfortune to be heterosexual will find it difficult to signal her availability and interest except through a conventionally feminine self-presentation. The stakes here are high: unless a woman can sell herself successfully in the heterosexual "meat market," she risks the loss of male sexual attention, sexual release, and emotional intimacy that, for better or worse, she is seeking. While feminist theory might prefer to ignore them, these needs in heterosexual women can be *imperious*. It is also the case, at least in the middle class, that if a woman can attract a wage-earning husband or lover, her standard of living will normally rise.

Consider now the pleasures of normative femininity. The disciplines have multiple meanings, both social and personal. So, for example, while high-heeled shoes are, to my mind, the modern equivalent of foot-binding, the occasion of getting one's first pair is an important rite of passage into adulthood. Memories, often poignant, longing, and the pleasures of female bonding cling to the disciplines. Many body rituals and the camaraderie that surrounds them are important occasions for feeling solidarity with other women. Unless new forms of female solidarity appear, women will be loathe to abandon the forms they know.

Mastery of the disciplines, like other sorts of mastery, requires knowledge, practice, patience, and the acquisition of skill: any suggestion, then, that the disciplines weren't worth the trouble it took to acquire them may well bring on resentment as well as the resistance of any artisan to de-skilling.

Femininity is also importantly an aesthetic; men and women alike cling to what they take to be beautiful, especially in the absence of an alternative. What alternative aesthetic of the body do feminists propose to put in place of the one that now holds sway? This is one reason (there are others) why the image of the feminist for so many comes to be associated with that of the "bull dyke." If feminists, enemies of glamour, do not want to be women, i.e., to look and act like proper women, then it follows that they must want to look and act like men.

What pleasure there is in drawing upon oneself the gaze of admiration or desire! The power of allure changes the odds in the battle of the sexes, albeit temporarily. This may well be the most power a woman will ever exert, at least in her dealings with other adults; no wonder that this moment, the moment in which she attracts or fascinates, is repeated over and over again in the romance novel. In catching the reflection of myself in the admiring glance of the other, I fuse my gaze with his and enjoy myself as he enjoys me. But there are more straightforward narcissistic pleasures at work in the production of femininity, pleasures of a sort that are not permitted men. Constant attention to the body—brushing the hair, anointing oneself with creams and lotions, soaking in a tub of foam—these are surely occasions of auto-eroticism. Like all narcissists, we are fascinated by our image; hence the scopophilia that makes it impossible to pass a mirror without looking (however, the sight of our facial skin in the harsh light above the dental chair may produce scopophobia!). The fashion-beauty complex does the impossible: it addresses our narcissistic needs and at the same time covertly assaults our narcissism, creating a sense of lack that only its products can fill. The pleasures of self-love are balanced by the pain of self-hatred. The pleasures of femininity, like the pleasures of smoking, are purchased at too high a price: the trick here may be to figure out how to get the pleasure without paying the price.

And then there are the sorts of situations in which rebellion against the prevailing semiotics of embodiment will involve behavior in which the political appears to come into conflict with the ethical. The occasions that constrain us the most to exhibit normative femininity are occasions of great ceremony and often solemnity, e.g., weddings and funerals. The fact that this is so, I think, serves importantly to underscore in people's minds the necessity and appropriateness of the caste hierarchy described by Frye. Now I could strike a blow against the system by appearing at Uncle John's funeral or Cousin Sara's wedding in overalls and boots. No one would understand my statement: some would take my appearance as a sign of disrespect. Indeed, the coercion at work on me here *not* to strike a blow against femininity is precisely that in so doing I *would* be showing disrespect. In such situations, unless I dress as other women dress, I call attention to myself and I do so under circumstances in which calling attention to myself is just wrong. Uncle John or his grieving family should be the focus of attention at his own funeral, clearly I and my politics should not. I may disapprove of the conventionalities of Cousin Sara's wedding; if my disapproval is really profound, I should stay away. But if I go, Sara and her groom should be the ones on whom all eyes are fixed, not me. Here, "doing the right thing" is at the same time a kind of blackmail.

I come finally to what it is that ties us perhaps most securely to this system: our identities. The norms of feminine body discipline are not imposed upon fully formed subjects; they are importantly implicated in the very construction of our subjectivities. Hence, while femininity may be a performance, here actor and role—while not identical—are highly fused. To have a body felt to be feminine, i.e., a body constructed through the appropriate practices, is crucial in most cases to a woman's sense of herself as female and, since, in the binary system in which we appear to be trapped, to her sense of herself as an existing individual. To possess such a body may also be essential to her sense of herself as a sexually desiring and desirable subject. If my analysis is correct, then any political project which aims to dismantle the machinery that turns a female body into a feminine one may well be apprehended by a woman as something that threatens her at best with desexualization, at worst with outright annihilation.

Postmodernist feminism has taught us, however, that identity is never unitary, i.e., fully self-consistent, also that identities or aspects of identities are often acquired under protest. Moreover, the "discourses"—the disciplines and practices—within which our identities are constructed are multifarious and often contradictory. So, in learning that we must become "feminine," we also learn (officially) that we are the equals of men, a proposition that appears, to say the least, compromised by many aspects of feminine body display. In this society, we learn too that we are to be responsible agents, that we must cultivate our individuality and that we are, finally, self-determining. Again, the ethical structures contained within these discourses sit uneasily alongside the conformist and ambiguously demeaning "subtext" of the discourse of femininity. The contradictory discourses within which our subjectivities are constituted may well contain within themselves the possibility of resistance.

IV. Resistance and Transformation: What Is to Be Done?

In spite of the seductions of femininity, there is, from some, resistance. Perhaps the mass audience for Naomi Wolf's *The Beauty Myth* are potential resisters. Female bodybuilders are resisters; they impose upon themselves another discipline, one that offends against the aesthetic of femininity. The younger women who work in the financial district of Chicago take off their pumps at the end of the day and wear running shoes on the bus home: in a small way, they too are resisters. Cross-dressers and drag queens are, ambiguously, resisters. Women who take self-defense courses and study martial arts are resisters. Women in radical lesbian communities are resisters: size is not regarded with disgust; moreover, aging in these communities is sometimes seen to enhance a woman's sexual allure, not to signal its disappearance. Some radical lesbians have adopted modes of self-presentation that are original, expressive, and not imitative either of the more austere garb of many of their sisters or the conventional feminine body display of the conventionally heterosexual. Participants in the "big and beautiful" movements that ask us to re-vision large bodies as beautiful bodies are also resisters. My cousin in the suburbs, a happily married wife and mother, spends a weekend each year with her old sorority sisters. They rent a suite in a hotel and "let themselves go," spending most of the time lying about in comfortable bathrobes, laughing, sharing secrets, re-creating the camaraderie of college days. They neither make up their faces nor worry about their hair. They eat what they please. While my cousin is telling me about this yearly ritual, the very memory of it sets her face aglow. I think that what she values about this reunion is not only the renewal of friendship, but the extraordinary feeling of freedom it gives her. For two days a year, my cousin and her friends are resisters.

These resistances, what do they amount to? Are these resisters like termites invisible to the landlord who will one day bring down the house of discipline? I do not know the answer to this question; however, this is the most compelling topic in feminist philosophy of any I teach, especially for the younger women in my classes. They express profound dissatisfaction and even confess having suffered greatly from the pressures to be beautiful and especially thin. These young women have practiced the discipline and everything that comes with it as a fate, without the political analysis I try to provide. One-quarter of my female students have suffered from bulimia; their detailed accounts of what it is like to live with this (hiding it from parents or boyfriends) I found shocking, especially the damage done to the body by frequent vomiting. This hostility toward the "beauty myth," even as it enslaves, reminds one of the silent dissatisfaction of myriads of housewives in the fifties who suffered from Betty Friedan's "problem with no name." This malaise, shortly afterward, took an overtly political character.

When the women's movement is in a position to go once more on the offensive, it must develop as part of its cultural politics, a new politics of the body, an invention of new "styles of the flesh." I doubt that a genuinely novel politics of the body can come about within a consumerist capitalist society; unless the mode of production within which we transform ourselves is itself radically transformed, a new aesthetic of beauty would become nothing but an opportunity for the development of new disciplinary practices. Hence, more is required than "gender bending" or parodies of conventional gendered presentations of self, valuable though these strategies may be. Cultural change of the sort I envision rarely comes about as the result of deliberate strategy. (We think here of the failure of Amelia Bloomer's nineteenth-century dress reform movement.) Transformations in the ways that people envision and present themselves come in the midst of large cultural and political upheavals; often, they appear, as if spontaneously, after such upheavals. Nevertheless, the development of a radical new politics of the body must become part of the cultural politics of the women's movement and of other related movements, such as the movement to end gay and lesbian oppression. The difficulties of developing a revolutionary aesthetics of the body should not be taken as a declaration of the impossibility of freeing the imagination for new ways of revisioning the corporeal self.

I have seen this happen in my own time, first in the imaginative unisex inventions of the hippies, later in the Black liberation movement. This movement addressed not only economic and political issues but the low self-esteem that was tied to the inferiorization of African-American bodies. "Black is beautiful," they said, and it became beautiful. Dark skin and kinky hair were no longer occasions for shame but marks of pride. The Afro became at once fashionable and revolutionary. Those in the Black community today who wear African dress and jewelry, dreadlocks, or corn rows, have kept this tradition alive, but here, as in the cases I discussed earlier, departures from the norm carry a price. New revisioning took hold then, a circumstance that informs my analysis and feeds my hopes.

The transformation of bodies and identities that must be part of a cultural politics of the future will require altered modes of sexual desire and a new aesthetic, a new sensibility that can undertake a radical revisioning of the body. This revisioning will extend our conceptions of physical beauty—in both males and females—far beyond the narrow limits within which they are now confined: this new aesthetic will be more democratic and more inclusive than the exclusionary aesthetic that now holds sway.

In that distant society that exists now only in imagination, self-presentation will encourage fantasy, play, invention, and experimentation. Since people will be free, they will of course be free to refuse ornamentation on behalf of austerity or utter simplicity. Presentations of self will no longer be constrained by the necessity of announcing one's gender, for the emergence of a revolutionary aesthetic of the body will announce the actual or immanent demise of the gender system. Presentations of self will no longer be constrained by the necessity of broadcasting one's class because class will be on its way out as well. The radicalization of beauty norms can, I believe, come about only in a radically democratic society: radical democracy as I understand it is incompatible with class society. As this society of the future comes more and more to value diversity, self-presentation will reflect this, both in the affirmation of one's own cultural heritage and, insofar as this is possible and appropriate, in the sharing of racial and cultural markers. It is futile to try to imagine very concretely how the inhabitants of this post-revolutionary society will revision their bodily selves, for they will do this freely, unconstrained by the sophisticated disciplinary regimes that are so inescapable a fixture of the current cultural landscape.

Notes

1. Interiors can also be "masculine" or "feminine": my brother's bedroom with its burlap walls, dark plaid bedspread, and football pennants was decidedly masculine, mine, with its canopy bed, white organdy ruffles, and rose-flecked wallpaper, decidedly feminine.

2. Electrolysis consists in inserting a needle into the hair root and then sending down an electric current which will kill it. Electrolysis is expensive and painful. To my knowledge it is the only method of permanent hair removal.

3. Nevertheless, if one did everything recommended in any issue of *Vogue* or *Cosmopolitan*, there would scarcely be time to do anything else.

Works Cited

Bartky, Sandra Lee. 1990. *Femininity and Domination*. New York: Routledge.

Beauvoir, Simone de. 1974. *The Second Sex*. New York: Vintage Books.

Bordo, Susan. 1995. "Anorexia Nervosa: Psychopathology as the Crystallization of Culture." *Philosophical Forum* 16, no. 2 (winter).

———. 1995. *Unbearable Weight: Feminism, Western Culture and the Body*. Berkeley: University of California Press.

Butler, Judith. 1985. "Embodied Identity in De Beauvoir's *The Second Sex*." Unpublished manuscript, presented to American Philosophical Association, Pacific Division, March 22.

——. 1990. *Gender Trouble: Feminism and the Subversion of Identity*. New York: Routledge.

Chernin, Kim. 1981. *The Obsession: Reflections on the Tyranny of Slenderness*. New York: Harper and Row.

Foucault, Michel. 1979. *Discipline and Punish*. New York: Vintage Books.

Frye, Marilyn. 1983. *Politics of Reality: Essays in Feminist Theory*. Freedom, Calif.: Crossing Press.

Henley, Nancy. 1977. *Body Politics*. Englewood Cliffs, N.J.: Prentice-Hall.

Klinger, Georgette, and Barbara Rowes. 1978. *Georgette Klinger's Skincare*. New York: William Morrow.

Loren, Sophia. 1984. *Women and Beauty*. New York: William Morrow.

Millman, Marcia. 1980. *Such a Pretty Face, Being Fat in America*. New York: Norton.

Saffon, M. J. 1981. *The 15-Minute-A-Day Natural Face Lift*. New York: Warner Books.

Young, Iris. 1989. "Throwing Like a Girl: A Phenomenology of Feminine Body Comportment, Motility and Spatiality." In *The Thinking Muse: Feminism and Modern French Philosophy*, Iris Young and Jeffner Allen, eds. Bloomington: Indiana University Press.

CHAPTER TWO

~

Agency: What's the Problem?

I

Agency: what's the problem? Bodies of theory that have wide currency at the present time appear to deny that we have it—that's the problem. The various poststructuralisms (and some of the structuralisms) have been taken by many if not most commentators to deny the reality of agency, as we ordinarily understand agency. These bodies of theory proclaim "the death of the subject" and hence, appear to deny the reality of subjectivity as we ordinarily understand subjectivity.

An "agent" is someone who is contemplating an action, has already acted or is presently acting. But "action" *tout court* is not incompatible with the agent's being wholly determined by factors outside her control. Hence, the sense of "agency" that appears to be threatened by the poststructuralisms (and some structuralisms) must involve action of a particular sort—action that is self-generated or self-determined, action that arises as a consequence of an agent's (or subject's) having chosen so to act.[1] Agents or subjects that can act freely are called "moral agents" or "moral subjects" by philosophers: a moral agent is someone whose actions can be evaluated according to moral criteria, i.e., whose deeds can be vicious or virtuous, praiseworthy or blameworthy. The moral evaluation of the actions of a subject assumes not only the freedom, hence the responsibility of the one acting, but, in addition, the rationality and maturity of this subject as well. I have regarded myself as a subject in this sense: Have the reports of my death been exaggerated?

The poststructuralisms (and some structuralisms) claim, or appear to claim, that I am wholly constructed within the dominant discourses and practices of my society, that I am an "effect" of "regimes" of power/knowledge, that my identity has been constituted within the phony binarisms of Western philosophy, that I am not someone who produces texts so much as someone produced by them, that I am hopelessly fractured—far too fractured ever to fit the description of the moral agent offered above, having left behind important parts of my "self" when I entered the Symbolic (culture), that I myself have been "interpellated" or "called forth" by the dominant ideology, i.e., that not only are my beliefs forms of ideological mystification, but so is my very sense of myself as a rational and autonomous individual.[2]

The hoary problem of free will vs. determinism will not be gainsaid: here it is again. There is more at stake here than questions about the freedom and hence the moral accountability of individual subjects; the possibility of radical political transformation appears to be threatened as well. If the least sympathetic critics of poststructuralism are correct, then the political subject who dreams that she is sufficiently free, in concert with other political subjects, to bring into being an even freer subject in a free society is just deluded. Since it is impossible in a short space to examine all the major poststructuralists, I shall focus in what follows on one exemplary poststructuralist: Michel Foucault. I shall argue that there is nothing in Foucault's account of the social construction of the subject that threatens the concept of agency or compels us to abandon, in principle, the idea of a subjectivity free enough to build a freer society.

There are two major schools of Foucault interpretation: the one posits a "bad Foucault" who puts forward a theory of the subject that, in effect, denies the possibility of political agency, hence of meaningful political betterment, the other a "good Foucault" who is himself a rebel against the existing order of domination and whose work is intended merely to warn us of the limits and dangers that are attendant upon projects of social amelioration. Clearly, the "good Foucault" poses no threat in principle to the possibility of moral or political agency.

The final two volumes of The History of Sexuality are clearly written by the "good Foucault." Here, Foucault looks to the ancient world to find models of individuals (privileged male individuals) who were able freely to give shape and form to themselves, especially to their sexual selves, this self-making often in line with aesthetic criteria.

However, the great works on which Foucault's reputation rests, namely, The History of Sexuality, Vol. 1 and Discipline and Punish seem to tell a different story; here subjects are formed largely from without not from within. The

most effective critics of the "bad Foucault" have argued that Foucault's conception of the subject is incoherent in that it tacitly assumes in the course of
critique what it explicitly denies. Now if Foucault's theory of the subject is
incoherent, as these critics claim and if Foucault's theory of the subject is, in
effect, a critique of agency as agency is ordinarily understood, it fails, for an
incoherent critique of agency is no critique at all. In the next section, I shall
examine a version of the "bad Foucault," in the one following, the "good
Foucault." In the final section, I shall offer some observations of my own that
bear on Foucault interpretation and hence on the question of agency.[3]

II

While Peter Dews' compelling *Logics of Disintegration* takes issue with Foucault's concept of the subject, Dews finds much in Foucault's reading of the
nature of modernity which is challenging, provocative and with which he is
clearly in agreement. I have no quarrel with Dews' exposition of Foucault's
ideas; hence I shall merge my exposition with his and turn to Dews' specific
critique of Foucault later in this section.

Foucault claims that from the onset of modern times, the state was committed to forms of administration and the provision of welfare that were unknown in feudal Europe and which led to increasingly invasive forms of social and psychological control (Dews, 146–47). Hence, the Age of
Enlightenment gave birth not only to modern democratic institutions and to
the idea of inalienable human rights, but also to multiple projects of control,
new and unprecedented disciplines that targeted the body in order, ultimately, to gain control of the mind.

Power in feudal societies could be exercised in ways that were quite brutal; nevertheless, this power was haphazard and inefficient; much of civil society lay beyond its reach. The monarch—image and embodiment of
power—was a public personage. The king was known, but his subjects were
largely unknown; his power was exercised on a largely anonymous body of
subjects. Foucault argues that the transition to modern society involved "a
reversal of the political axis of individualization."[4] What this means is that
the effects of power in modern societies "circulate through progressively finer
channels, gaining access to individuals themselves, to their bodies, their gestures, and all their daily actions."[5] As the project of control cannot go forward without the knowledge of how to control effectively, the emerging "human sciences" are thus forms both of knowledge and power, "regimes" of
"power/knowledge" enlisted in the service of what Foucault calls the "disciplinary" or "carceral" society. The bureaucratic mode in which power is

exercised becomes increasingly faceless and impersonal. Everyman, however, loses *his* anonymity; everyone becomes a case—a case in the file of some bureaucracy.

Many of the disciplinary practices that Foucault associates with modernity antedate modernity, but they are taken up, refined, and expanded in the peculiarly modern forms of the army, the asylum, the school, the hospital, the prison, the factory, and the family. The new disciplinary practices require that an uninterrupted coercion held in place by constant surveillance be directed to the very processes of bodily activity; a "microphysics" of power partitions the body's time and its space; it regiments the body's posture, gesture, and motility and requires a minute and precise articulation of the body's relationship to such instruments as the rifle, the school desk, or the machine (DP, 28).

> A "political anatomy" which was also a "mechanics of power," was being born; it defined how one may have a hold over others' bodies not only so that they may do what one wishes, but so that they may operate as one wishes, with the techniques, the speed and the efficiency that one determines. Thus, discipline produces subjected and practiced bodies, "docile" bodies. (DP, 139)

Foucault's conception of the practice most indispensable to the creation of "docile bodies"—surveillance—is captured in the image of the Panopticon, Jeremy Bentham's design for a model prison, in which one jailer in a central tower watches many criminals displayed in windowed cells. The arrangement of windows, one facing outward, the other inward, allows an effect of backlighting that makes figures within the cell visible to the supervisor in the tower. "All that is needed, then, is to place a supervisor in a central tower and to shut up in each cell a madman, a patient, a condemned man, a worker or a schoolboy" (DP, 200). "Panopticism" resonates throughout society: it is no surprise then that "prisons resemble factories, schools, barracks, hospitals, which all resemble prisons" (DP, 228).

The effects of surveillance mechanisms directed initially toward the disciplining of the body get a hold on the mind as well; they induce a psychological state of "conscious and permanent visibility" (DP, 201). This perpetual surveillance is internalized, giving rise to that reflective self-awareness which is the hallmark of the individual in bourgeois society. The anonymity of the jailer's gaze from the tower is a metaphor for the impersonality of modern bureaucratic power. The shift from "juridical power" (the power of the monarch, priest, or judge) to the disciplinary power of modern administrative bureaucracies is paralleled by the shift from epic narrative to the modern literature of introspection and to the rise of philosophies of consciousness (Dews, 160).

According to Dews, Foucault is not pointing to the asymmetrical and inegalitarian features of modern society in order to urge upon us democratic reforms that would make possible a true self-determination. "Foucault's argument is that any theory of sovereignty or self-determination must be abandoned, since the 'free subject' upon which such theories rely is in fact intrinsically heteronomous, constituted by power" (Dews, 161). The disciplinary practices of modernity that construct the modern subject do not limit liberty, they are, says Foucault, "the *foundation* of the formal juridical liberties" (DP, 222). Hence, "the man described for us whom we are invited to free"—presumably in both older and newer discourses of liberation—"is already in himself the effect of a subjection much more profound than himself" (DP, 30).

Dews maintains that it is Foucault's aim to establish a direct and unequivocal relationship between "subjectification"—the production of subjects—and "subjection" (Dews, 16). This Foucault states explicitly in the first volume of The History of Sexuality: "Men's subjection: their constitution as subjects."[6] "Sexuality," says Foucault, "is the set of effects produced in bodies, behaviors and social relations by a certain deployment deriving from a complex political technology" (HS, 127). Sexuality has, of course, a biological basis, but as lived by specific historical subjects, it is a system of discourses and practices that "forms part of the intensifying surveillance and control of the individual which is Foucault's central historical theme" (Dews, 165).

The "deployment" of sexuality is not primarily repressive, for power can be productive of pleasure.[7] "Deployment" constructs subjects both through the incitement to desire and in the fixing of identities. One's identity is now thought to inhere in a core sexual self. The association of personal identity with the idea of a core sexual self is linked to the ritual of confession which migrates from the Church to the new human sciences, such as, e.g. psychoanalysis. This linkage illustrates nicely Foucault's claim that the constitution of subjectivity itself is an effect of oppressive social practices. Confession, be it religious or psychoanalytic, unfolds within an inegalitarian relationship, for one confesses to another who has authority not only to require the confession but also to determine whether the confession itself reveals a core self that is virtuous or vicious, mature or immature, normal or abnormal.

Dews is critical of Foucault on a number of grounds. While Foucault appears hostile to the technologies of domination he describes in such detail, the normative standpoint that informs this hostility is obscure. Foucault's rejection of Enlightenment humanism is well known: he cannot reject the

carceral society on behalf of a freedom to be won by a potentially free subject, if to be a subject at all is already to have been subjugated. The modern
subject is not the autonomous subject of liberal political theory; for Foucault,
such a subject is illusory. Remember: "Men's subjection: their constitution as
subjects." Dews claims that Foucault is unable to say "how a situation would
change if an operation of power were cancelled"; he cannot admit the possibility of such a "counterfactual" because he regards power as omnipresent,
not because it would have the privilege of gathering everything under its in-
vincible unity, but because it is produced at every moment, at every point or
rather in every relation between points" (Dews, 167).

The extraordinary looseness of this conception of power is tied to Foucault's lack of normative clarity. Dews regards this conception of power
("power is everywhere") as a vague metaphysical monism, a night in which
all cows are black. There is no longer anything determinate to which a power
so conceived could be opposed: moreover, if "effects" of power are productive
of desire, as Foucault argues in the *History of Sexuality*, the link between
power and oppression on the one hand and desire and liberation, on the
other, is severed. Differently put, this diffuse a conception of power removes
the teeth from any genuine critique of power.

To his diagnosis of the reasons for Foucault's lack of normative clarity,
Dews adds another damaging charge: this involves an alleged incoherence in
Foucault's conception of the subject. In spite of the pervasive and suffocating
presence of power everywhere in the social totality and in spite of his inability to say precisely what is wrong with modern disciplinary power, Foucault
maintains that "where there is power, there is resistance" (HS, 95). Resistance, moreover, "is never in a position of exteriority in relation to power . . .
points of resistance are present everywhere in the power network" (HS, 95).
What precisely are these "points of resistance"? If subjects are constituted
within disciplinary regimes of power, *who* is it that resists? Is the "who" that
resists not a subject? If not a subject, then what? Why is there resistance at
all? Why do some resist and not others? In a word, how is resistance possible?

There are passages in the *History of Sexuality* in which Foucault makes un-
explained reference to "the body and its pleasures" as an alternative to the
practiced and docile body brought into being by the "deployment" of sexuality. He yearns in one passage for an *ars erotica* in which, unlike the *scientia
sexualis*—the regime that now holds sway—pleasure would not be considered
"in relation to an absolute law of the permitted and the forbidden, nor by reference to a criterion of utility, but first and foremost in relation to itself"
(HS, 76). These references to the "body and its pleasures"—to what Dews
calls "the libidinal body"—a body that could somehow escape the network of

power relations and disciplinary practices—appears flatly to contradict the uncompromising theory of the social construction of the subject that Foucault develops in his most celebrated work.

So Foucault appears to be impaled on the horns of a dilemma. Either he abandons the high ground of an uncompromising social constructionism for some version of naturalism or biological essentialism—a move that would nullify his very premise in the *History of Sexuality*, i.e., the wrongness of sexual liberationist notions of a repressed natural sexuality (the "repressive hypothesis")—or else he is stuck with the incoherent notion of resistance without a resister, a totally untheorized resistance that is knowable only as the absolute Other to power and whose origins and basis lie shrouded in mystery.

III

I turn now to Jana Sawicki's admirable *Disciplining Foucault*, a feminist retrieval of the "good Foucault," a Foucault whose theory of the subject should hold no terror for female agency or for feminist politics. There are gaps, admits Sawicki, in Foucault's account of the genesis of the modern subject: focusing on the microstructures of power, he is not sufficiently attentive to its macrostructures. Sawicki admits Foucault's lack of normative clarity. Nevertheless, she believes that Foucault's project is compatible with values such as "justice, liberty and human dignity" (Sawicki, 11). While Sawicki is aware that Foucault sometimes writes as if the hold of disciplinary power were total, she reminds us too of Foucault's claim that "resistance and struggle are co-present with power and that power is continually transformed in the face of such resistance" (71). Sawicki cites a late interview with Foucault:

> I'm not positing a substance of power. I'm simply saying: as soon as there's a relation of power there's a possibility of resistance. We're never trapped by power: its always possible to modify its hold, in determined conditions and following a precise strategy.[8]

Foucault's model of the social field is of a myriad of shifting relations, multiple centers of power confronting multiple centers of resistance. Sawicki understands this to mean that socialization is a theoretical project that is never completely realized in practice. Foucault does not see the relationship between society and the individual as one of univocal determination, but as one of ambiguity and conflict. Nor should we forget that "individuals are the vehicles as well as the targets of power" (64). Hence, Foucault's "social constructionism need not imply social determinism" (41). Nor does his social constructionism pose a principled threat to the reality of human liberty. Again Sawicki supports her reading of Foucault with a citation from another late interview: "Power is exercised only over free subjects and only insofar as they are free."[9] The meaning of Foucault's work for Sawicki is primarily procedural and methodological. His rejection of the atomic, asocial individual of Enlightenment political theory and of theories that posit an authentic human nature can free us for new forms of subjectivity. This is particularly important for feminism, since a strong case can be made that the most influential theories of human nature have been androcentric. While Foucault himself is generally neglectful of gender, his genealogies, i.e., his inquiries into the origin and development of power/knowledge regimes can, by revealing their contingency, free us from their influence; again, these inherited regimes are androcentric. Foucault's genealogical method is also designed to facilitate an "insurrection of subjugated knowledges"—forms of knowledge that "have been disqualified as inadequate to their task, or insufficiently elaborated: naive knowledges located low down in the hierarchy, beneath the required level of cognition or scientificity."[10] These are the voices of the odd, the mad, the delinquent, the silenced, and the different. They are the voices of women, *our* voices. But Sawicki finds in Foucault's conception of a knowledge/power regime and in its other, subjugated knowledge, a cautionary tale for feminists: the white, middle-class bias of much feminist theory reveals the power of the relatively advantaged to ignore the "subjugated discourse" of the less advantaged. Without any conscious intent to introduce a racism of omission into feminist writing, what was supposed originally to be the articulation of a subjugated discourse can turn out to function as a hegemonic discourse, i.e., as an instrument of domination.

Feminist theory is linked indissolubly with theories of sexuality and in Foucault's theory of the social construction of the sexual subject, Sawicki again finds cautionary tales for feminists. While Foucault does sometimes speak as if the "domain of sexuality were already colonized beyond redemption," he understands sexuality as we must understand it too: neither wholly outside nor yet wholly circumscribed by power, it is an arena for struggle wherein there are no "inherently liberatory or repressive sexual practices" (43). Feminism has produced its own deployment of sexuality: it too has generated normalizing discourses that attach individuals to particular identities, deviation from which bespeaks a low level of consciousness or worse, the scandal that one isn't "really" a feminist. Showing far better political sense than Foucault himself, Sawicki defends "identity politics" in a society that persecutes those it has already attached to stigmatized and despised identities. In the same vein, she quite rightly defends the practice of consciousness-raising as a feminist strategy against Foucault's critique of the confessional.

One methodological feature of Foucault's work that Sawicki especially admires is his nuanced analysis both of the subtle forms of social control that are at work in the "micropolitical" encounters of everyday life and of the "deep regularities and broad and impersonal forces that make us what we are" (99). A knowledge of these anonymous historical processes can give us a certain critical distance on our own sensibilities: such knowledge should not lead to a denial of rational agency but to a more secure understanding of its parameters, its possibilities, and its limits.

IV

Here then are two very different readings of Foucault. Whose Foucault is the real Foucault? The "bad Foucault" whose theory of the social construction of the subject within networks of power denies the possibility of agency, autonomy, and liberation from domination ("men's subjection: their constitution as subjects") or the "good Foucault" who does not deny the reality of liberty and whose aim it is merely to refine and historicize our understanding of agency ("Power is exercised only over free subjects and only insofar as they are free")? For our purposes, it matters not whose Foucault is the "real" Foucault. If Dews' reading is correct, Foucault's theory of the making of the modern subject is both implausible and incoherent: the implicit critique of agency contained in so flawed an account of the processes of "subjectification" need detain us no longer. If Sawicki's reading is the right reading, then Foucault has added important new theoretical dimensions to our understanding of agency. Either way, agency is saved.

It is difficult to leave this topic without some comparison of two such contradictory interpretations of the same thinker. In some ways, such a comparison is misleading: Dews is far more concerned to attack Foucault than Sawicki is to defend him. She searches out in Foucault's work what feminists, especially, can find useful in it; she raids the master's tool box.[11] Nor does Sawicki hesitate to take Foucault to task both for his androcentrism and for his political pessimism. Sawicki's project, as I understand it, is to show that Foucault's methodology is compatible with a political framework that continues to privilege the Enlightenment values of "justice, liberty and human dignity." She does, however, offer a general interpretation of Foucault's work that is, on balance, in line with the use she wishes to make of him. Sawicki's Foucault is a philosophical libertarian concerned principally to identify the mechanisms that suppress our liberty.[12]

Part of the problem lies with Foucault himself. Many of his pronounce-ments in interviews given after the publication of the central texts that es-tablished his reputation seem flatly to contradict the tenor and direction of these earlier texts. Furthermore, as I shall argue below, there are two quite different models of the functioning of power at work in these major texts. What appear to be disparities between the late interviews and the positions Foucault takes in his major texts bespeak, for some, flexibility, a refreshing lack of dogmatism and the courage for constant intellectual innovation. For others, these disparities betray fundamental, indeed fatal, inconsistencies in his thought; when faced with these inconsistencies, it is as if Foucault were saying, "That is not what I meant, not what I meant at all."

Peter Dews' Foucault interpretation relies on the major texts of Foucault's maturity—*Madness and Civilization, The Birth of the Clinic, Discipline and Pun-ish, The History of Sexuality,* Vol. 1—in which the constitution of the modern subject is spelled out in some detail, while a substantial number of Sawicki's citations are to interviews given by Foucault after the appearance of the main body of his work, indeed, after the emergence of the sorts of criticisms of his work that are elaborated in Dews' text. In one of his last interviews, Foucault speaks of liberation, a topic strikingly absent from his central texts:

> I do not mean to say that liberation or such and such a form of liberation does not exist. When a colonial people tries to free itself of its colonizer, that is truly an act of liberation, in the strict sense of the word. But as we also know . . . this act of lib-eration is not sufficient to establish the practices of liberty that later on will be nec-essary for this people, this society and these individuals to decide upon receivable and acceptable forms of their existence or political society.[13]

The phrase "practices of liberty" and the clear implication in this passage that political freedom is not only desirable but possible sounds strange issu-ing from the great enemy of Enlightenment. The same late interview yields another surprising observation:

> I don't believe that there can be a society without relations of power if you under-stand them as means by which individuals try to conduct, to determine the behav-ior of others. The problem is not of trying to dissolve them in the utopia of a per-fectly transparent communication but to give one's self the rules of law, the techniques of management, and also the ethics, the *ethos*, the practice of self, which would allow these games of power to be played with a minimum of domination.[14]

Here, the "relations of power" have been radically demoted: in the great works on which Foucault built his reputation, power does not just "try" to determine the behavior of others, it succeeds in constructing the very subjec-tivity of the subject—her self-consciousness, her desire, and her identity—the "truth of her being." The self that here gives itself the rule of law seems unlike the docile, practiced, and self-policing subject of *Discipline and Punish* and quite like the Kantian self whom Foucault has been thought to have buried. Nor is there anything in this passage that can explain why a self, or a community of selves capable of giving *themselves* "rules of law" would still have to suffer a "minimum of domination."

Sawicki cites with approval Foucault's claim that "where there is power, there is a resistance." But this seems flatly false: certainly the exercise of power is very often consented to or colluded in. Moreover, neither Sawicki nor Foucault seem able to meet Dews' challenge: If power does indeed create identities and shape desires, *who* is it that resists? Whence comes the desire to resist? What are the origins of this resistance? What are its motives?

I want to argue now that there are *two* quite distinct models of the opera-tion of power at work in Foucault's texts. In addition to the apparent lack of fit between many of Foucault's most influential works and his late interviews, there is a more serious lack of fit between Foucault's differing understandings of the nature and operations of power. Foucault's own conflation of these models gives rise, I believe, to the problem about the nature, identity, indeed, the possibility, of the one who resists the imposition of power.

On the first model, power is the maker of persons. Power is productive and its products are specific forms of historical subjectivity. Since Foucault rejects the claim that there is anything like a human nature that is transhistorical in character, power on this model has in effect a *tabula rasa*—the individual, not yet a subject—on which to inscribe its various constructions. But power so conceived appears to differ very little from socialization. Indeed, Sawicki ex-pressly identifies power as producer of persons with "socialization" (41). But socialization is a largely descriptive, not a normative notion. If the power that is productive of subjects is no more than socialization in disguise, then Foucault's critique of the "carceral society" loses all force. His treatment of modern disciplinary power, however, is thoroughly critical in tone even while the basis of this critique remains obscure, hence his famous lack of "normative clarity." Sawicki can find Enlightenment values in Foucault—"justice, liberty and human dignity"—because these values function as the suppressed, indeed the denigrated, premises of his argument.[15]

The second model of the functioning of power is not that of power as per-son-maker but of power as one player in a social field—really a battlefield—where multiple centers of power confront multiple centers of resistance. Saw-icki: "Power circulates in this field and is exercised on and by individuals over others as well as themselves" (25). When asked in an interview who it is that struggles against whom, Foucault answers in a manner worthy of Hobbes:

> This is just a hypothesis, but I would say its all against all. There aren't immediately given subjects of a struggle, one the proletariat, the other the bourgeoisie. Who fights against whom? We all fight against each other. And there is always within each of us something that fights something else.[16]

Dews' objection to Foucault's claim that "power is everywhere" is, in my view, vindicated: power conceived in so diffuse a fashion loses its role in an effective political critique. A host of different modes of conflict, some external, some internal, are here distilled into one brew: Dews' "vague metaphysical monism." A bad metaphysics appears to have crept into the picture, certainly a bad politics. "We all fight against each other": How would this sit with the victims of sexist or racist violence? How would it sit with countless workers made "redundant" by "crises of profitability" who, because of "welfare reform," lack even the debilitating expectation that they may well spend the rest of their "immediately given" lives on the dole? Power cannot make us at once the subjected subjects of the carceral society and the antagonists on a Hobbesian "darkling plain" of ceaseless strife.

I end with several cautionary notes of my own. While Sawicki is undoubtedly correct in valuing Foucault's account of "deep regularities" and "broad and impersonal forces" in history, his account is by no means the premier account of such forces. Foucault's attitude toward Marxism is consistently ambiguous: at times he attacks it, at other times patronizes it and sometimes he is at pains to show its continuity with his own work. We should not lose sight of the fact that the various Marxisms have produced detailed and impressive bodies of theory that lay out not only the "deep regularities" and "broad historical forces" in history (regularities and forces to which Foucault pays little attention) but offer accounts as well of the ways in which these forces have structured institutions and generated subjectivities.[17] In my view, we ignore these bodies of theory at our peril.

Foucault is less ambiguous and more openly hostile toward psychoanalysis. While I do not think that a version of psychoanalysis has yet appeared that satisfies fully the requirements of an adequate critical theory, I doubt that without it, we will be able to understand unconscious processes, their relationship to identities, especially to gendered identities, and to the macrosystems of domination that now hold sway. Foucault's accounts of "subjectification" are original and compelling, but they need to be supplemented by at least this "human science," whatever its historic entanglement in projects of domination. Once again, we ignore the search for an adequate political psychology at our peril.[18]

Fashions in theory change: Foucault and other poststructuralists such as Derrida and Lacan are currently in vogue. But we must remember that long before Foucault's writing had found an audience here, indeed, long before Foucault had written many of the works on which his fame chiefly rests, feminists of the Second Wave had already produced an impressive critical analysis of the micropolitics of everyday life, the normalizing practices of masculinity and femininity, the compulsory imposition of identities, and the regimes of knowledge and power that sat like toads on our own emerging but still subjugated discourse. Early on, what many regarded as a subjugated discourse was found to be, by virtue of its unintended racism, a discourse that subjugated others. This discovery was not made by studying the texts of structuralists or poststructuralists but in the context of political struggle—a struggle waged by feminists of color (and some white feminists) against the myopia of a largely white-dominated feminist theory and practice; what was and still is being struggled for is a multiracial, cross-class movement that can bring into being a freer society of freer agents. The discourse that has emerged from this struggle and from struggles around such things as age, class, and sexual preference is feminist discourse too; it is theory linked to practice which, in turn, is animated by a utopian vision. "Where there is no vision, the people perish." Where there is no vision, a political movement may die as well. It is a tribute to Foucault's influence that we find ourselves so often using his terminology to describe what it was we were doing and indeed are doing still. But Foucault's dystopia of skirmish and counter-skirmish, of "all fighting each other" into an indefinitely prolonged future is not our vision. Even though they are flawed, indeed flawed in ways we have yet to realize, we have powerful and original political and intellectual traditions of our own: we ought to honor them.

Notes

This chapter was previously published in Provoking Agents: Gender and Agency in Theory and Practice, edited by Judith Kegan Gardiner (Urbana: University of Illinois Press, 1995).

1. For purposes of this chapter, I shall take "agent" and "subject" to be synonymous.

2. The theories alluded to here are, in order, those of Foucault, Derrida, Lacan, and Althusser.

3. Commentators who find a significant degree of incoherence in Foucault's theory of the subject include: Peter Dews, Logics of Disintegration (London: Verso, 1987)—hereafter "Dews"; Michael Walzer, "The Politics of Michel Foucault and Charles Taylor," "Foucault

on Freedom and Truth," both in *Foucault, A Critical Reader*, ed. David Hoy (New York: Basil Blackwell, 1986); Nancy Fraser, *Unruly Practices: Power, Discourse and Gender in Contemporary Social Theory* (Minneapolis: University of Minnesota Press, 1989); Frederic Jameson, "Postmodernism, or, the Cultural Logic of Late Capitalism," *New Left Review* 147 (September 1984). Feminist critics who find Foucault's theory of the subject incompatible with feminist politics include Susan Bordo, "Feminism, Postmodernism and Gender-Skepticism" and Nancy Hartsock, "Foucault on Power: A Theory for Women?" both in *Feminism/Postmodernism*, ed. and intro. Linda Nicholson (New York: Routledge, 1990). See also Nancy Hartsock, "Rethinking Modernism: Minority vs. Majority Theories," *Cultural Critique* 7 (fall 1987); Linda Alcoff, "Feminism and Foucault: The Limits to a Collaboration," in *Crises in Continental Philosophy*, eds. Arleen Dallery and Charles Scott (New York: State University of New York Press, 1990); and Barbara Christian, "The Race for Theory," *Cultural Critique* 6 (spring 1987).

Some defenders of the "good Foucault" include Paul Rabinow, Introduction to *The Foucault Reader*, ed. Rabinow (New York: Pantheon Books, 1984); David Hoy, Introduction and "Power, Repression, Progress: Foucault, Lukes and the Frankfurt School," also Richard Rorty, "Foucault and Epistemology," all in *Foucault, A Critical Reader*. Some feminist critics who find Foucault's theoretical framework useful for feminism include Jana Sawicki, *Disciplining Foucault* (New York: Routledge, 1991) (see extended discussion below); Irene Diamond and Lee Quinby, Introduction and "American Feminism and the Language of Control," in *Feminism and Foucault*, ed. Diamond and Quinby (Boston: Northeastern University Press, 1988). In the same volume see Biddy Martin, "Feminism, Criticism and Foucault," and Mary Lydon, "Foucault and Feminism: A Romance of Many Dimensions."

4. Michel Foucault, *Discipline and Punish* (New York: Vintage Books, 1979), 44. Hereafter DP.

5. Michel Foucault, *Power/Knowledge*, ed. Colin Gordon (Brighton: Harvester Press, 1980), 151. Cited by Peter Dews, "Power and Subjectivity in Foucault," *New Left Review*, no. 144 (March–April 1984), 17.

6. Foucault, *The History of Sexuality*, Vol. 1 (New York: Vintage Books, 1978), 60. Hereafter HS.

7. See, however, "'Catch Me if You Can': Foucault on the Repressive Hypothesis" in this volume (chapter 3).

8. Michel Foucault, "The History of Sexuality: An Interview," trans. Geoff Bennington, *Oxford Literary Review* 4, no. 2 (1980), 13, cited in Sawicki, p. 25.

9. Michel Foucault, "The Subject and Power," Afterword in Hubert Dreyfus and Paul Rabinow, *Michel Foucault: Beyond Structuralism and Hermeneutics* (Chicago: University of Chicago Press, 1982), 221, cited in Sawicki, p. 25.

10. Michel Foucault, Introduction to *Herculine Barbin: Being the Recently Discovered Memoirs of a Nineteenth Century French Hermaphrodite* (New York: Pantheon, 1980), 126, cited in Sawicki, p. 26.

11. See, e.g., "Foucault, Femininity and the Modernization of Patriarchal Power," in Sandra Bartky, *Femininity and Domination: Studies in the Phenomenology of Oppression* (New York: Routledge, 1990).

12. See esp. her footnote 18, p. 125: "The subject presupposed in Foucault's later discourses resembles the creative, nihilating subject found in the writings of French Existentialist, Jean-Paul Sartre."

13. "The Ethic of Care for the Self as a Practice of Freedom: An Interview with Michel Foucault on January 20, 1984," in *The Final Foucault*, ed. James Bernauer and David Rasmussen (Cambridge: MIT Press, 1988), 12–13.

14. Ibid., 18, cited in Sawicki, p. 124.

15. The same point is made in a paper by Isaac Balbus, "Disciplining Women: Michel Foucault and the Power of Feminist Discourse," in *After Foucault: Humanistic Knowledge, Postmodern Challenges*, ed. Jonathan Arac (New Brunswick: Rutgers University Press, 1988), 138–160.

16. Foucault, *Herculine Barbin*, 208, cited by Sawicki, p. 25.

17. See, for example, Samuel Bowles and Herbert Gintis, *Schooling in Capitalist America* (New York: Basic Books, 1976); Richard Sennett and Jonathan Cobb, *The Hidden Injuries of Class* (New York: Vintage, 1973); Reimut Reiche, *Sexuality and Class Struggle* (New York: Praeger, 1971); Michael Schneider, *Neurosis and Civilization* (New York: Seabury Press, 1975); Eli Zaretsky, *Capitalism, the Family and Personal Life* (New York: Harper and Row, 1976); Bertell Ollman, *Social and Sexual Revolution* (Boston: South End Press, 1979). Ollman writes very perceptively of the earlier work of Wilhelm Reich, which, while flawed in many ways, attempts to understand character formation in terms of the intersection of the micropolitics of the family with the macrostructures of capitalism. See, for example, Wilhelm Reich, *Sex-Pol: Writings 1929–1934*, ed. Lee Baxandall, with an Introduction by Bertell Ollman (New York: Random House, 1972). While their Marxism is very unorthodox, much of the work of the Frankfurt School belongs in this category as well. See for example, Theodor W. Adorno, Else Frenkel-Brunswik, Daniel J. Levinson, R. Nevitt Sanford, *The Authoritarian Personality* (1950; reprint, New York: John Wiley and Sons, 1964). See also Max Horkheimer, "Authoritarianism and the Family," in *The Family: Its Function and Destiny*, ed. Ruth Anshen (New York: Harper and Brothers, 1949). The remarkable work of Herbert Marcuse should be mentioned in this connection as well: see *Eros and Civilization: A Philosophical Inquiry into Freud* (New York: Vintage Books, 1962). In *A History of Sexuality*, Vol. 1, Foucault consistently underplays his indebtedness to Marcuse and Reich.

18. For an account of what such a psychology would entail, see Dorothy Leland, "Lacanian Psychoanalysis and French Feminism: Toward an Adequate Political Psychology," in *Revaluing French Feminism: Critical Essays on Difference, Agency and Culture*, ed. Nancy Fraser and Sandra Bartky (Bloomington: Indiana University Press, 1991).

~

"Catch Me if You Can": Foucault on the Repressive Hypothesis

I. The Repressive Hypothesis

Foucault's assault in *History of Sexuality*, Vol. I, on what he calls the "repressive hypothesis" is widely regarded as a major theoretical advance in our understanding of sexuality and as one of the chief ornaments of Foucault's thought. I want to challenge this judgment; I shall argue that some of Foucault's reasons for urging us to jettison the repressive hypothesis fail to persuade. I want to argue too against Foucault's "dumbing down," i.e., his rather egregious misrepresentation of the views of those influential twentieth-century theorists who put forward some version of the repressive hypothesis, namely, Freud, Reich, and Marcuse.

First of all, what exactly does Foucault take the repressive hypothesis to be?

> For a long time, the story goes, we supported a Victorian regime and we continue to be dominated by it even today. . . . At the beginning of the seventeenth century a certain frankness was still common, it would seem. Sexual practices had little need of secrecy, words were said without undue reticence and things were done without too much concealment. . . . But twilight soon fell upon this bright day, followed by the monotonous nights of the Victorian bourgeoisie. Sexuality was carefully confined; it moved into the home. The conjugal family took custody of it and absorbed it into the serious function of reproduction. On the subject of sex, silence became the rule. . . . These are the characteristic features attributed to repression which serve to distinguish it from the penal law: repression operated as a sentence to disappear, but also as an injunction to silence, an affirmation of nonexistence

and, by implication, an admission that there was nothing to say about such things, nothing to see and nothing to know. (Foucault 1990, 3–4)[1]

Having said this, Foucault at once qualifies it: the Victorians knew that "infernal mischief" could not be made to disappear entirely; hence the mental hospital and the brothel, the prostitute and the pimp, the neurologist and his hysteric. According to the repressive hypothesis, the general regime of repression is adjusted to coincide with "the development of capitalism; it becomes an integral part of the bourgeois order" (5).

The repressive hypothesis also has a powerful utopian moment: the idea of liberation from repression. The project of liberation calls for an overthrow of the sexual status quo in which a new set of discourses and practices will link "sex, the revelation of truth, the overturning of global laws, the proclamation of a new day to come and the promise of a certain felicity" (7). It should be noted here that "repression" as Foucault understands it is something that is supposed to happen to conscious agents only as a consequence of conscious beliefs and practices. This is not the way the idea of repression is commonly understood. As far as I know, "repression" found its first expression in the work of Sigmund Freud, for whom it covers a wide range of unconscious activities. I will return to this point later.

Foucault poses three questions ("serious doubts") to the repressive hypothesis: (1) "Is sexual repression truly an established historical fact" (10)? In the course of answering this question, it will become apparent that there are in fact two questions at stake here: first, is there really such a thing as sexual repression, at least as (according to Foucault) it has been traditionally understood? Second, is the chronology associated with defenders of the repressive hypothesis correct? As we shall see, Foucault will answer both questions in the negative. (2) Are the workings of power, in a society such as ours, generally repressive, repression being characterized as "prohibition, censorship and denial," elsewhere as "refusal, blockage and invalidation" (10–11)? This question is ambiguous. Given the multifarious forms that power can take, it might be the case that power operates differently in the sexual domain than it does in other orders of experience. So a more precise formulation of the question would be this: Does the regulation of sexuality *per se* take the form of "prohibition, censorship and denial?" Foucault answers this question in the negative as well. (3) Does the critical discourse that is addressed to repression by the repressive hypothesis represent a genuine challenge to it or "Is it not in fact part of the same historical network as the thing it denounces (and doubtless misrepresents)" (10)? The very wording of this question suggests the way in which Foucault will answer it. (See Section III below.)

Aware that the position he is developing runs counter to received opinion, Foucault tries to set the perplexed reader straight: "I do not claim that sex has not been prohibited or barred or masked or misapprehended since the classical age, nor do I even assert that it has suffered these things any less from that period on than before" (12). The points that Foucault would like to score against the repressive hypothesis "are aimed less at showing it to be mistaken than at putting it back within a general economy of discourses on sex in modern societies" (11). So Foucault's predecessors were on to something but they got it wrong. But did they, in fact, get it wrong?

II. Catch Me if You Can!

If censorship and silence are part and parcel of repression, says Foucault, then how to explain the "veritable discursive explosion" around issues of sexuality of the last three centuries (11)? Foucault concedes that "a whole restrictive economy" was introduced into the "politics of language" throughout society at large (18). But this seems far less important to him than the claim that "the multiplication of discourses" both issued from and was taken up by the "agencies of power" (18).

Now the Reformation encouraged everyone to be on the lookout perpetually for impurities in thought, word, or deed. Many Protestants (as we know from their diaries) were tormented by sexual thoughts and sinful desires they could not seem to expunge from consciousness. When Calvinists acceded to state power in places like Geneva or Puritans in the Massachusetts Bay Colony, they established highly sexually repressive theocracies. But these are not histories that Foucault mentions, much less relates. Staying closer to home, i.e., France, he tells us that the Counter-Reformation attributed ever more importance to "insinuations of the flesh" (19ff). Foucault cites a pastoral letter of the period:

> Examine diligently, therefore, all the faculties of your soul: memory, understanding, and will. Examine with precision all your senses as well. . . . Examine moreover all your thoughts, every word you speak, and all your actions. Examine even unto your dreams, to know if, once awakened, you did not give them your consent. (20)[2]

Now we learned in *Discipline and Punish* that surveillance, especially unrelenting surveillance and of course self-surveillance, is profoundly disempowering: it is part of the production of "docile bodies"; it is, in a word, "repressive." The Puritan theocracies as well as the clergy of both the Reformation and Counter-Reformation tried to put entire populations under a stricter surveillance than they had known before. We would expect too the same strongly implied condemnation of sexual repression here as Foucault offers of the disciplinary practices of modernity in *Discipline and Punish*. Has Foucault changed his mind about the inextricability of surveillance and domination?

An "explosion of discourse" (albeit in language Foucault grants is extremely circumspect) occurs in such fields as biology, pedagogy, medicine, later criminology, sociology, anthropology, psychology, psychiatry—the "human sciences." Insofar as censorship and silence are crucial to repression, an explosion of discourses having to do with sex, it seems to Foucault, is surely at odds with the repressive hypothesis. But how can we ignore the fact that there was a discursive explosion—due to the rapid dissemination of print media in virtually every field? Foucault offers no evidence whatsoever to support the claim that in proportion to the total volume of publication, sexual matters get more attention than they had gotten—again, in proportion to total volume—in the Middle Ages. One can argue, of course, that late in this period, psychology and especially psychoanalysis, in which there does appear to be an "explosion" of discourse, are very much discourses about sexuality. But psychoanalysis, especially in its initial phases, is a renegade discourse, what Foucault sometimes calls "a subjugated knowledge" whose aim, in part, is to discredit other, more established discourses.

Seen in historical context, are the sexual discourses that appeared in the eighteenth and nineteenth centuries in any way unique? There was a passion during this period for the close observation and classification of all sorts of natural phenomena. Foucault recognizes that modern states come increasingly to require information as to the constitution, health, and augmentation of their populations; the authorities require knowledge in order to exercise "biopower." But once again, are we dealing here with a unique phenomenon? During this period, instrumental rationality was brought to bear on every aspect of endeavor, from the improvement of productive techniques, to the control of populations and the radical reform of institutions. Foucault does not provide us with statistics or even a bibliography in support of his claim that there was a unique and disproportionate "explosion of discourse" concerning sexuality or a project of bio-control that differs in any important way from the "disciplinary practices" so meticulously described in *Discipline and Punish*.

It should be noted too that the texts of pedagogy, medicine, etc. circulated within an extremely small circle of specialists—mainly white, privileged, European or Euro-American men. This information was not conveyed to the general public, many of whom, in the earlier phases of the modern period, were illiterate. When, in college, I tried to inform myself about sexual "perversions," I discovered that the sexually explicit passages in Krafft-Ebing were all in Latin. My high-school trek through Caesar's *Gallic Wars* was insufficient. "Sex was driven out of hiding and made to lead a discursive existence" (33). One is tempted to add "a discursive existence, for those who knew medical Latin." I take it that most of the discourses to which Foucault appeals have scientific pretensions as well as the overt or covert aim of controlling sexuality. The application of science (or pseudo-science) to the project of controlling sexual behavior sounds more like ammunition for the repressive hypothesis than evidence against it.

Even if we grant, for the sake of argument, that there was, in the eighteenth and nineteenth centuries and down to our own time, an inordinate amount of talk and text dealing with sexuality, this fact, if fact it is, is not incompatible with the claim that sexual repression was, on balance, the order of the day. First of all, not everyone was authorized to speak or to write about sex. Texts produced by scientists for other scientists were allowed; after all, they typically justified, directly or indirectly, the regulation of sexuality. Novelists had no such freedom. As late as 1890, the British censor banned Tolstoy's *Resurrection* from the mails as it portrayed a prostitute sympathetically. Journalists and feminists had to struggle for the right to discuss openly important social issues such as prostitution. W. T. Stead, British journalist and author of *The Maiden Tribute of Babylon*, a high-minded exposé of "white slavery," containing neither sexually explicit language nor explicit descriptions of sex acts, was nevertheless prosecuted by the Crown. Similar charges but a worse fate—terms of imprisonment—awaited those, like Margaret Sanger, who distributed birth-control information. Second, it may be the case that sexual repression scars the soul so badly that when one finally wins the right to free expression, there springs the hope that speech or writing can be healing. It mostly cannot; hence the need for more speech and more writing. The obsessional preoccupation with sexuality that Foucault believes to be characteristic of modernity in the West may well be the discursive equivalent of the tongue's irresistible attraction to an aching tooth, or to the equally irresistible need to scratch at one's scabs. What he calls the "garrulousness" concerning sexuality in modern times is not incompatible with sexual repression.

But what was happening in the larger society while Foucault's "authorities" on sexuality were busily producing and consuming texts? What, in particular, was going on with children? Any evaluation of Foucault's critique of the repressive hypothesis must take into account the sexual socialization of children, for the patterns laid down in childhood are implicated in the formation of character, hence they are notoriously difficult to alter in adulthood.

The lack of censorship that allowed a few "experts" (normally in the name of science) to publish on sexual matters is quite different from the society-wide sexual censorship that was imposed on children and, in the milieu in which I was raised, most adults.

As childhood sexual socialization varies greatly historically and also by race, class, ethnicity, and nationality, no comprehensive account has yet appeared or is likely to appear.[3] I therefore offer some typical features of my own childhood sexual socialization, for three reasons: first, much of what I relate will be familiar to Foucault's readers, especially his older readers; second, while I was raised in Chicago in the 1940s and 1950s, I might just as well have been brought up in Freud's Vienna of the1890s; finally, my sexual upbringing was what, before Foucault, virtually anyone would have called "repressive." What was happening to ordinary children in the familiar sites of social life during Foucault's "discursive explosion"?

Sex, for middle-class girls of my generation, was not driven out of hiding; whenever it threatened to appear, it was driven massively *into* hiding. We were forbidden to explore our bodies, indeed, we were not taught the proper names of our private parts; we were forbidden to engage in sex-play with other children, to masturbate, or to utter words relating to sexual matters. These things were not only forbidden, they were punished. Sex was never mentioned in my home, nor was there sex education in our schools. Sex was—not just a secret, but The Secret.

My first menstruation occurred when I was quite young; as I had no idea what was happening to me, I was terrified, believing that I was bleeding to death. The day this happened, my mother told me only that now I mustn't let a man touch me for I could get pregnant. I was quietly skeptical of this, knowing how often men brushed against women on the bus, especially during rush hour. I knew that all those women didn't go home and get pregnant, though I had no idea then or for years afterward, how women did get pregnant. My father mumbled something to me that evening in acknowledgment of the event, but we were both too embarrassed to discuss it then and it was never mentioned again. While I knew next to nothing about human sexuality, I knew enough to be ashamed: I was covered in shame at the prospect that my father or brother might see traces of this monthly ordeal; I wrapped and removed used sanitary napkins surreptitiously from the bathroom so that they could be buried in the anonymity of the kitchen garbage. Four lonely years passed before I heard two schoolmates whispering about "it." I felt inexpressible relief in finding friends who got "the curse" every month, too. Keeping secrets can be a lonely business. As menstruation is a female affair, my very femaleness was implicated in my shame and in my need for secrecy.

The association of sex with what was dirty or filthy was then and is now a cultural given. There were "dirty jokes," "filthy pictures," and "dirty old men." The British, I learned later, speak of "dirty (i.e., adulterous) weekends." One would expect that a historian of sexuality would clarify—or at least notice—this association; why the absence of any discussion in Foucault's genealogy of modern sexuality of the pervasive identification of sex with dirt and filth?

Now a Foucaultian would be entirely unimpressed by my sad little childhood tale. Have I not become still another "confessing animal," typical of one who complains of sexual repression (censorship, denial, etc.) and then offers an intimate and uncensored narration ("Western Man has become a confessing animal" [59])? My reply to this is to set my story of the workings of sexual prohibition against a story of Foucault's. The passage is worth quoting at length:

> The medical examination, the psychiatric investigation, the pedagogical report, and family controls may have the over-all and apparent objective of saying no to all wayward or unproductive sexualities, but the fact is that they function as mechanisms with a double impetus: pleasure and power. The pleasure that comes of exercising a power that questions, monitors, watches, spies, searches out, palpates, brings to light, and on the other hand, the pleasure that kindles at having to evade this power, flee from it, fool it, or travesty it. The power that lets itself be invaded by the pleasure it is pursuing and opposite it, power asserting itself in the pleasure of showing off, scandalizing, or resisting. Capture and seduction, confrontation and mutual reinforcement . . . all have played this game continually since the nineteenth century. These attractions, these evasions, these circular incitements have traced around bodies and sexes, not boundaries not to be crossed, but *perpetual spirals of power and pleasure*. . . . The power which thus took charge of sexuality set about contacting bodies, caressing them with its eyes, intensifying areas, electrifying surfaces, dramatizing troubled moments. It wrapped the sexual body in its embrace. There was undoubtedly an increase in effectiveness and an extension of the domain controlled; but also a sensualization of power and a gain of pleasure. (44–45)[4]

Foucault has now answered two of his original questions. The kind of power that is brought into play against bodies is not primarily repressive: it "intensifies areas, electrifies surfaces . . . wraps the sexual body in its embrace." Foucault is here claiming that increased surveillance in the modern period had the effect of heightening pleasure, though he does not clarify the mechanisms at work. However, he makes clear in the same passage that the analysis holds good for all sexual regulation, not just for the rooting out of sexual irregularities. The game of "capture and seduction" is played by "parents and children, adults and adolescents, educator and students, doctor and patients" (45). The point that Foucault will drive home over and over again is the productivity of the power that prohibits. In addition to erotic incitement, this power produces new knowledges and new social types.

If prohibition is regularly eroticized, as Foucault claims in this passage, then there is nothing in this state of affairs that corresponds to the way in which Foucault defines repression. We recall that for Foucault, repression is supposed to shut down sexuality, cancel it, annul it; a prohibition that incites, that excites both the one who surveys and the one who is put under surveillance is no kind of repression at all. "'Sexuality' is far more a product of power than power was ever repression of sexuality."[5] I myself find it difficult to accept the claim that domination (and the power of which Foucault speaks is a project of domination) is, for most people, regularly eroticized. If it were, then if we wanted full and rich sex lives we would campaign against, for example, sex education in the schools, punish children's sex play, etc.[6] At any rate, Foucault's conclusion is clear enough: "We must therefore abandon the hypothesis that modern industrial societies ushered in an age of increased sexual repression" (49) and later in the same text, "It appears unlikely that there was an age of sexual restriction" (122). Foucault underscores this claim elsewhere:

> The notion of repression is quite inadequate for capturing what is precisely the productive aspect of power. In defining the effects of power as repression, one adopts a purely juridical conception of such power, one identified power with a law which says no, power is taken above all as carrying the force of prohibition. Now I believe that this is a wholly negative, narrow skeletal conception of power, one which has been curiously widespread. (Foucault, *Politics, Philosophy, Culture*, 119)[7]

Foucault's story is considerably less depressing than mine. Indeed, he describes a perpetual game of "Catch Me if You Can." The constant preoccupation with watching is eroticized for the regulator, while for the one regulated, there is the "pleasure of showing off, scandalizing, or resisting" (45). For me there was no pleasure in showing off; the sense of taboo that attached to all things sexual both at home and at school hung over me so heavily that the punishments I anticipated from its violation were terrible, even though they were never articulated clearly. No pleasure was kindled in me at having to evade this power. What I have described—bits and pieces only of a much longer and even sadder tale—is not a story of "perpetual spirals of power and pleasure." My surfaces were not electrified nor as far as I knew, was my body wrapped by power in a sexual embrace: on the contrary, the point was to hide and keep hidden from authority all things pertaining to sex. There was no "sensualization of power" and certainly no "gain of pleasure"; indeed, I believe that the effect upon me of sexual taboo was, overall, an erotic loss of considerable dimensions.

The *kind* of regime toward which my story points is far more typical (especially for women) than Foucault's exciting game of "Catch Me if You Can." He writes of titillation but not of pain. The profound absence at the heart of *History of Sexuality*, Vol. I, is the shame and guilt that is associated with sexuality in the minds of countless individuals whose sexuality was silenced, annulled, circumscribed, even proscribed, tabooed, punished, made shameful, and guilt-ridden. Where is the recognition of shame in this text, where is the theorization of guilt? There is no acknowledgment that the sexual repression of children is responsible for much sexual suffering in adults. Prohibition and injunctions to hide are not, of course, limited to childhood. There are, for example, large numbers of homosexual adolescents who are even more at risk of suicide than at-risk heterosexual adolescents. There are homosexual adults who are forced to live the lie that they are heterosexual, in constant fear of exposure, hence of shame and the rejection by their families, the possible loss of livelihood and, in some states, criminal prosecution. Theoreticians of the repressive hypothesis had much to say about sexual shame and sexual guilt. I shall argue in the next section that Foucault presents a radically impoverished account of the more influential versions of the repressive hypothesis. This stacks the deck against Foucault's theoretical rivals; also, in my opinion, it obfuscates the entire issue of sexual regulation.

III. "I Know a Secret"

Foucault ascribes to theorists of the repressive hypothesis the view that repression is nothing but the "affirmation of (the) non-existence" of sex. This affirmation is buttressed by silence, prohibition, censorship, nullification, denial, or taboo. The repressive hypothesis puts forward only an "emaciated form of prohibition. . . . It never establishes any connection between power and sex that is not negative: rejection, exclusion, refusal, blockage, concealment or mask" (88). His view, on the contrary, is that the power that came to be exercised over sexuality is productive—of "perpetual spirals of power and pleasure," of new knowledges (e.g., psychiatry), of new identities (the pervert, the homosexual, the nymphomaniac).

The idea that Freud, Reich, and Marcuse believed that the effects of repression were merely negative and unproductive is flatly false. Knowledge and pleasure are, for Foucault, the results of sexual prohibition that defenders of the repressive hypothesis are said to ignore. But how can anyone at all familiar with Freud overlook the fact that for him, the phenomenon of sexual repression, in all its complexity, is indeed a source of new knowledge about the human psyche? New pleasures are identified by Freudian discourse as well, e.g., anal eroticism.

Moreover, Freud, as every schoolchild knows, believed that sexual repression is productive of (pause here for emphasis) *civilization*! How much more productive can anything get?

> it is impossible to overlook the extent to which civilization is built up upon a re-nunciation of instinct, how much it presupposes precisely the non-satisfaction . . . of powerful instincts. This "cultural frustration" dominates the large field of social relationships between human beings.[8]

And elsewhere, in the same passage from *Civilization and Its Discontents,*

> Sublimation of instinct is an especially conspicuous feature of cultural development, it is what makes it possible for higher psychical activities, scientific, artistic or ideological, to play such an important part in civilized life.[9]

Furthermore, for Freud, Reich, and Marcuse, shutting down, nullifying, prohibiting, etc., sexual feeling is *impossible* because all believe that sexual energy is a crucial dimension of the human organism: dammed up in one place, it will find new channels in which to flow; denied satisfaction of its original object of desire, it will substitute (sublimate) another. Now none of this should be interpreted as in any way a defense of Freud's instinct theory, or of his ideas concerning "the vicissitudes of the instincts" or of his claim that civilization is based on sexual repression. My aim here is solely to expose Foucault's gross misreading of Freud.

Moreover, quite apart from the merits or demerits of instinct theory, it seems to me that Freud has a concept of repression that is more complex and intellectually sophisticated than Foucault's truncated version. For Foucault, repression is interpersonal. Other people, acting in accord with prevailing discourses and social practices, exercise upon me a series of "deployments" whereby my sexuality is "constructed" in ways that are specifically modern. For Freud, on the other hand, repression is both interpersonal and intra-personal. The prohibitions that originate with external authorities are internalized: repression becomes something that I do to myself. Tabooed desires as well as an elaborate internalized repressive apparatus—the Censor or Super-ego—keeps these desires at bay even while it allows them some disguised expression. Many of my desires as well as my Censor or Superego are largely un-conscious, in spite of the fact that they determine critical aspects of my be-havior and personality. Foucault's rejection of psychoanalysis is so total that nowhere in *The History of Sexuality*, Vol. I, is there any suspicion that impor-tant dimensions of our sexual ideas or sexual desires might be unconscious. This results in impoverished portraits of those whose "deployment" of sexu-ality socially constructs the sexual self as well as those selves targeted by the same "deployment."

Let us return to Foucault's example of one site in the genesis of "spirals of power and pleasure," the secondary schools of the eighteenth century (72–73). Let us imagine a monitor who patrols the halls and peeps through small glass windows in the boys' rooms to see if they are mastur-bating. It is Foucault's contention that there are two pleasures at work here: the pleasure the boys must take in outwitting the monitors and the pleasure of the monitor, himself, "a pleasure that comes of exercising a power that questions, monitors, watches, spies, searches out" (44). Osten-sibly, the pleasure of the monitor consists in his contribution to the extir-pation of a prohibited sexual act; it is, by his own lights, the kind of plea-sure that one takes in performing moral actions. But neither we nor Foucault are so naive as to believe that this is the whole story. The mon-itor is excited by his proximity to acts that are, in his own eyes, sinful; he is able to indulge a forbidden, but fascinated voyeurism that secretly, in-deed unconsciously, is excited by the very thing that it condemns. He is titillated by prohibited behavior in the very act of prohibiting it. He may very well have sought out such a position in order to persist in his own bad faith; he lacks what most philosophers think is essential to the moral life, i.e. even a rudimentary understanding of his own motives. Indeed, if his unconscious enjoyment of "sin" were somehow to burst into conscious-ness, the monitor's psychic economy might be shattered. His is a pleasure that dare not know its name.

Foucault speaks simply of "pleasure" in his discussion of "spirals of pleasure and power." But there are all kinds of pleasures. There are pleasures so threat-ening to the individual that they can be enjoyed only in the act of rooting them out of others. There are guilty pleasures, pleasures that remain in the darkness of the unconscious because they are powerfully suffused with feel-ings of guilt, shame, and fear. The masturbating schoolboy must endure, we may assume, a large portion of guilt, shame, and a sense of sin as the price of his pleasure. Once again, one is struck by the absence in Foucault of any recognition of how troubled sexual pleasure can be precisely because of its at-tempted repression.

Wilhelm Reich, like Freud, believes in the productivity of sexual repression. Reich, Freud, and Marcuse believe that the working of repression in modern societies creates certain character types, a view that Foucault himself endorses. According to Reich, the character structures that have come into being in our sexually repressive regime help to reproduce the class structure of capitalism, hence the exploitation of human labor that produces wealth in class societies. Reich, in his earlier years, believed that sexual repression, in particular the prohibition of sexual play and exploration among children, and the denial of the compelling sexual needs of adolescents are ways to break the spirit.

> [C]apital defends the maintenance of sexual repression with all at its disposal . . . 1. It is a powerful prop of the church, which, with the assistance of sexual anxiety and guilt feelings, is deeply anchored in the exploited masses. 2. It is a prop of the institutions of family and marriage which require a stunting of sexuality for their existence. 3. It requires children to obey their parents, and prepares for the later obedience of the adults to the authority of the state and capital by producing fear of authority in all individuals in society. 4. It lames the critical intellectual powers of the oppressed masses. Sexual repression consumes a great deal of psychic energy that otherwise would be utilized in intellectual activity. 5. It damages the psychic ability of an immense number of people. It creates inhibition and cripples the power to rebel in materially oppressed individuals.[10]

Now there is a great deal here that no one today would want to defend. But it seems absurd to say that for Reich, sexual repression is nothing but a denial, a shutting down, a censoring, a taboo. While Reich may well be mistaken, it is a fact that he believed repression to be an important factor in the maintenance of an entire system of social relations, a powerful and resilient economic structure and powerful institutions that still dominate most people's lives.

Foucault takes Reich to task for errors in Reich's periodization of his account of repression. One would expect, on Reich's analysis, that first and foremost, in the early modern period, "the young adult man, possessing nothing more than his life force, had to be the primary target of a subjugation destined to shift the energy available for useless pleasure toward compulsory labor" (120). But this is not what happened. Indeed, it took several centuries to bring the working classes into line. (Foucault's admission that whatever the chronology, sexuality was eventually "deployed" against the workers appears to be a significant concession to Reich.) "The most rigorous techniques were formed and, more particularly, applied first, with the greatest intensity, in the economically privileged and politically dominant classes" (120). The sexual economy of the rising bourgeoisie was concerned with its own "vigor, longevity, progeniture, and descent" (121). The significance of the body of the bourgeoisie differed markedly from that of the landed aristocracy. The latter justified its rule in part on the basis of "blood," i.e., on the purity of its lineage. The former, as befits a militant rising class, was anxious to keep its youth from squandering its energies and vital bodily fluids in debaucheries that come increasingly, in the public mind, to expose the decadence of the aristocracy, hence its unfitness to rule. The close monitoring of its sexual substance, a saving that requires self-mastery and self-control, worked, at least in its own eyes, as a moral justification of the bourgeoisie's accession to power. Finally, however, Foucault and Reich are not so far apart after all. Foucault did not believe that capitalism produces the discourses and practices it needs; rather, local practices and policies arise for a variety of reasons: the ones that serve the needs of the bourgeoisie survive; the rest do not. The eventual success of the sexual repression of the working class, though it differs from place to place in character and quality, is sufficiently widespread to conclude that it must indeed serve the interests of the bourgeoisie. Foucault makes what can as easily be regarded as a contribution to Reich's analysis as a critique of it, namely, the idea that sexual repression can play itself out differently in different classes:

> If it is true that sexuality is the set of effects produced in bodies, behaviors and social relations by a certain deployment deriving from a complex political technology, one has to admit that this deployment does not operate in symmetrical fashion with respect to the social classes, and consequently, that it does not produce the same effects in them. (127)[11]

It should be noted that what I continue to call "sexual repression," since I am not convinced that this term can or should be abandoned, Foucault begins to call "sexuality" or "the deployment of sexuality" in the last half of *History of Sexuality*, Vol. I. Hence, his claim that "sexuality is originally, historically bourgeois" (127). This sounds strange to our ears; nevertheless, it is the case that the term "sexuality" did not come into general use until the nineteenth century. Having diagnosed (or narrowed and misdiagnosed, as I have been arguing) the concept of "repression" as erroneous and misleading, Foucault turns to a terminology that will do, more or less, the same work. The choice of the term "deployment," with its military echoes, suggests that there is more going on than mere sexual regulation. But military metaphors capture neither the anguish that has deformed the sexuality of so many in late modernity nor the joy that has sometimes attended its liberation.

Finally, Marcuse.[12] Like Freud, Marcuse accepts an instinct theory: like Foucault he believes that individuals resist the imposition of sexually repressive regulation (Foucault believes that individuals tend to resist the imposition of disciplines *tout court*). Whatever the status of the instinct theory, Marcuse can at least offer an explanation for this resistance—its instinctual basis; Foucault cannot. Both thinkers are hostile to normalization in the sphere of sexuality. Marcuse rejects Freud's claim (and Reich's), that only heterosexual genitality is psychosexually normal: he is drawn to another model of sexuality, "polymorphous perversity," i.e., the re-eroticization of those parts of the body whose sexual sensitivities, according to the Freudians, have to be repressed to allow the "normal" adult to focus on genitality. This is echoed by Foucault's plaintive call for a return to "bodies and pleasures."

> It is the agency of sex that we must break away from, if we aim—through a tactical reversal of the various mechanisms of sexuality—to counter the grips of power with the claims of bodies, pleasures and knowledges, in their multiplicity and their possibility of resistance. The rallying point for the counterattack against the deployment of sexuality ought not to be sex-desire but bodies and pleasures. (157)

Ladelle McWhorter interprets this rather obscure passage in the following way: "Sex-desire" refers to sexual identity, a concept that carries too heavy a weight of normalization, i.e., too many norms that are thought to cling necessarily to particular identities. In the antihumanist tradition of postmodernism, Foucault imagines a state of affairs whereby individuals, no longer modern subjects constructed along disciplinary lines, are free to explore the multiplicity of bodies and pleasures. "Sex is the linchpin of sexuality; desire is sex-desire. The desiring subject, thoroughly normalized, is the sexual subject. Affirmation of desire, even in the plural, will do nothing to undermine the *dispositif de sexualite*."[13]

While Marcuse believes in the existence of a core sexual self, this self may be deeply buried, never, for want of opportunity, to see the light of day. The core self may be nothing but a potentiality; what shows itself is socially constructed according to what Marcuse calls "the established order of domination." The parallels between Foucault's utopia of "bodies and pleasures" and Marcuse's "polymorphous perversity" are evident, as is the idea that the subjectivities we are have been constructed in conformity to an exploitative regime.

Reich's conception of sexual repression has been historically superseded by a far more permissive sexual regime that now allows (in some of its incarnations) sexual behavior that was disallowed in Reich's day—premarital intercourse, abortion, homosexuality, pornography, etc. Foucault recognizes this phenomenon and the ways it too can be "repressive" but he does not pursue this issue theoretically.

The lifting of taboos has not ushered in a period of sexual satisfaction. The commodification that is so prominent a feature of capitalism invades consciousness, especially the consciousness of embodiment and both men and women try to package themselves for success in the "meat market." Billions of dollars are spent each year for toning and exercising the body, on diets, makeup, clothes, plastic surgery, etc. Since women are still the primary targets of sexual objectification, it is women who are the major consumers of products and services that will presumably make them deserving of male attention. This regime, as I have argued elsewhere, creates in contemporary women low self-esteem and a very specific set of anxieties about embodiment (that can turn pathological, as in bulimia or anorexia nervosa).[14] Now insofar as older taboos have been lifted, there has occurred a "de-sublimation," to use a term of Marcuse's, but this de-sublimation is still repressive, only in new ways. So contemporary sexuality is importantly, for Marcuse, as it is for feminists, a "repressive de-sublimation." Foucault is widely admired for having brought to sexual theory the idea that sexuality as well as subjectivity is "socially constructed." But, as I have suggested, this idea was developed earlier, both by Marcuse and by feminist theorists; indeed, one can trace the rather detailed development of this notion, at least in reference to subjectivity, to Simone de Beauvoir. And John Stuart Mill had argued in *On the Subjection of Women* that it would be impossible to know what woman's true nature in fact is, until the current "social construction" of the female character is abolished. Until recently, however, feminists stopped short of the Foucaultian claim that the deep or core self, our roles and representations, as well as our biologies, are socially and historically constructed.

While Reich believed that sexual repression was necessary only for the perpetuation of capitalism, Marcuse takes the more conservative view that there is a certain "necessary" repression required by an organized and productive social and economic life; he believed that the requirements of capitalism (and, as he later admitted, patriarchy) require "surplus repression." Hence, repression is not just nugatory; like Reich, Marcuse believed that it produced and reproduced the central features of contemporary social life in the "developed" societies. Since Marcuse believed in the possibility of an overthrow of macrosystems of domination (with varying conviction at different stages in his career) he is often optimistic about the possibility of a life free of "surplus repression," i.e., a much freer and happier sexuality. There is thus a utopian moment in Marcuse that is developed theoretically out of his analysis of repression and its relationship to advanced capitalism. This utopian moment is ridiculed by Foucault, even though he has his own utopian moment ("bodies and pleasures"), a moment that gets nothing more than a mere mention and whose normative status (given Foucault's resistance in this text to a ranking of discourses) is unclear.

While, as I have shown, Foucault is quite clear about the relationship between the bourgeois order and "the deployment of sexuality," this does not suggest to him (as it did to Marcuse) a strategy of liberation. While Foucault appears to have abandoned his agnosticism in regard to values in his discussions of Greco-Roman sexuality in Vols. II and III of *The History of Sexuality*, in Vol. I, he has been widely taken to be a relativist, seeing in history only a march of discourses and practices ("regimes of power/knowledge"), none of which will produce either an overarching truth or a liberated sexuality. Calvin Schrag's analysis of the consequences of Foucault's moral and epistemological relativism in the texts on which his reputation is based seems particularly apt here:

> Numerous challenges addressed to more traditional views of reason surface in Foucault's politics of power. If the logos is itself an effect of power, then any appeal to theory for a comprehension and management of the constraints of power would become useless. If the rational subject is product rather than an agent of power, then the grammar of autonomy and emancipation is deprived of any significant function. If everything, from our specialized disciplines of knowledge to our pre-reflective everyday practices, is imbued with power, there is neither resource nor standpoint to combat the specter of ideology that always hovers over the power relations in a given society.[15]

An instance of the relationship between power and truth, for Foucault, is the confession. The West for many centuries has believed that truth could be obtained through confession. This ancient belief, religious in origin, has been taken over by the manifold schools of psychology as well as by contemporary movements of sexual liberation:

> The obligation to confess is now relayed through so many different points, is so deeply ingrained in us, that we no longer perceive it as the effect of a power that constrains us; on the contrary, it seems to us that truth, lodged in our most secret nature, "demands" only to surface; that if it fails to do so, this is because a constraint holds it in place, the violence of a power weighs it down. (60)

Sex, "lodged in our most secret nature" constitutes the core, the veritable essence of the self and if this core can be articulated, truth will be revealed.

For Foucault, however, the idea that there is a sexual core that constitutes the essence of our being is not only a myth, it is part of the technology of subjugation developed within the deployment of sexuality. Foucault has now answered his third original question: Does the critical discourse that is addressed to repression represent a genuine challenge to it or "is it not in fact part of the same historical network as the thing it denounces" (10)?

Here, as in other postmodern texts, liberation discourse stands accused of essentialism. It is said to be equally bad to have a sexual essence ascribed to oneself (a core self) by others as to ascribe an essence to oneself. Ascriptions of this sort are always embedded in relations of power; "normalization" is here a principal weapon in the deployment of sexuality. Hence to be labeled a "queer," a "pervert," or a "slut" is to be exiled beyond the borders of normalcy; it is to be eternally defective in one's essence. Liberation movements remain, Foucault thinks, within the knowledge/power regimes that they are trying to combat: of Reich's vision, for example, he says "it always unfolded within the deployment of sexuality and not outside of it or against it" (131). Foucault is quite right about this. Reich agitated for a sexual revolution but regarded homosexuality as infantile and regressive.

But what of the modern gay rights movement itself? How vulnerable is it to Foucault's criticism? Movements for gay liberation accept the distinction between heterosexuality and homosexuality; they try only to valorize the persecuted partner in this duality. Hence, they have not gotten beyond a fundamentally oppressive way of carving up human sexuality; they have not broken through the "deployment of sexuality" to the freedom of "bodies and pleasures."[16] Furthermore, in its struggle to gain respectability for the movement, many of its participants stigmatize the flamboyance of swishers, cross-dressers, and drag queens. In this way, a liberation movement may create new norms that push to the margins some of those it ought to be liberating.

The history of Second Wave feminism tells a similar story (though it is hardly the main plot). It too has a history (in some, but not all of its manifestations) of exclusion and marginalization. Working-class women, women of color, and lesbians have complained that Second Wave feminism has either ignored them, or else failed to grasp the complex forms of oppression that are peculiar to their situation. Some lesbian separatists, in response, have declared sexual love between women or else celibacy to be the only legitimate choices for true feminists, hence marginalizing heterosexual feminists in a new discourse of normalization.

Since lesbian love was thought to be not only politically correct but more gentle, nurturant, and productive of true intimacy than heterosexual relations, the confessions of members of Samois, an organization of lesbian sado-masochists, that burst upon the scene in San Francisco in the late 1970s, were profoundly shocking to many lesbian—and heterosexual—feminists; lesbian sado-masochists were roundly condemned and entirely excluded by many (not all) from the community of "true" and "normal" feminism.[17] Examples of this sort could be multiplied at great length for both liberation movements, but I think that the general point is clear.

But Foucault's theoretical ambivalence in regard to these movements is somewhat short-sighted.[18] While political movements tend often to rehearse the very oppressive practices against which they are agitating, there is no comparison between the marginalization visited upon individuals by social movements and the marginalization and exclusion that is typically visited upon these same persons by the "established order of domination."

In spite of the flaws and deficiencies in social movements for sexual liberation, there is something about them that Foucault may have noticed but about which he has failed to remark. I refer to the life-altering and life-enhancing effect they have had on myriads of people. This "failure to remark" is an absence less striking than Foucault's failure to understand sexual misery but it bears resemblance to it: here that about which he fails to remark is joy. There is inexpressible relief in "coming out" or, as in women's consciousness-raising groups, "speaking bitterness." Joy and relief are proportional, perhaps, to the corrosive effects of having to live a lie at best, at worst, having to live under highly repressive circumstances, i.e., in fear of exposure, persecution, and disgrace. There is an extraordinary joy too in breaking out of the isolation that is imposed by rampant sexism and homophobia; why else would solitary confinement be the most dreaded punishment? The joy we feel in being thus released is a measure of our fragmentation and of the alienation from others we experience in everyday life; the joy of temporary escape is a measure of the unhappiness many feel for life in "normal" bourgeois society. Other girls bleed every month, not just me. Others have suffered what I have suffered: the "confessions" heard in these movements build solidarities among the participants and since every political movement needs solidarity, such confessions are empowering, not disempowering, as Foucault suspects are all confessions. In consciousness-raising and in "coming out," a renegade discourse takes shape. There is for many, an inexpressible joy in so speaking and in standing in solidarity with others, especially if one has felt, all her life, weak, defective, and despised. This joy is transformative: it releases the individual from the prisonhouse of personality—in which the disciplines (and their internalizations) have no doubt been inscribed—into a wider human arena. Foucault felt an extraordinary rush of solidarity during the early stages of the Iranian revolution. There is little indication in his published work that he knew the joys of solidarity closer to home.

It is inevitable that movements that challenge the established order will bear its stamp. While we need to hold tightly to our vision, insofar as we are persecuted, our persecutors determine in large measure our political agenda. Radically new regimes of power/knowledge cannot be invented out of whole cloth at the moment that antagonists of the established order recognize its bankruptcy. Typically, movements of contestation combine genuine innovation with elements that are older and more familiar. The polarities which structure current regimes of "truth" and power and in which contemporary social movements are imbricated—male/female, masculine/feminine, gay/straight, black/white, self/other—can, it is true, be deconstructed. Poststructuralist theory, critical race theory, queer theory—all have demonstrated the possibility of such an overcoming.[19] If all that Foucault is telling us, in his talk of the "deployment" of sexuality is that we must re-examine the terms and concepts with which we theorize our oppression and liberation, then he is certainly correct. But what Marx said of Hegel, namely, that he had overcome alienation in thought but only in thought is true here as well. Race, gender, and "sex-desire" may indeed be fictions but they have been overcome, if at all, only in thought; they structure the psychic and material reality of everyday life; we cannot cease to struggle against them, like it or not.

Notes

I would like to thank Isaac Balbus and William McBride for helpful comments on an earlier draft of this chapter. I would particularly like to thank Jana Sawicki, Ladelle McWhorter, and Elaine Miller for very detailed and careful critiques of the chapter especially as they reject the central claims I put forward here about Foucault and the repressive hypothesis.

This chapter was previously published in *Calvin O. Schrag and the Task of Philosophy after Postmodernity*, edited by Martin Beck Matuštík and William L. McBride (Evanston, Ill.: Northwestern University Press, 2002).

1. Unless otherwise indicated, all page references will be to Michel Foucault, *The History of Sexuality*, Vol. I (New York: Vintage Books, 1978).

2. Foucault's reference here is to Segneri, *L'Instruction du penitent* (n.p., n.d.), 301–2.

3. However, for a fascinating attempt to periodicize epochs of child-rearing in the West see Isaac Balbus, *Marxism and Domination: A Neo-Hegelian, Feminist, Psychoanalytic Theory of Sexual, Political and Technological Liberation* (Princeton, N.J.: Princeton University Press, 1983).

4. On the sexualization of domination, see also Foucault, *Politics, Philosophy, Culture* (New York: Routledge, 1990): "There is about sexuality a lot of defective regulations in

which the negative effects of inhibitions are counterbalanced by the positive effects of stimulation" (9).

5. Michel Foucault, *Power/Knowledge: Selected Interviews and Other Writings, 1972–1977* (New York: Pantheon Press, 1980), 120.

6. For a provocative account of the way in which severe childhood sexual repression may give rise to a fully masochistic sexuality, see Robert Stoller, *Perversion: the Erotic Form of Hatred* (London: Karmac Books, 1994), also his *Pain and Passion: A Psychoanalyst Explores the World of S and M* (New York: Plenum Press, 1991).

7. In spite of the apodicity of these statements, Foucault never articulates a fully coherent position on sexual repression. We must remember, in regard to the unconditionality of the first two statements above, that Foucault said earlier in the text that he did not want to deny the existence of repression so much as to recontextualize it. Yet, in the passages quoted, he does deny it. Nevertheless, he excoriates as "detestable" the press and popularizers of condensing his work into a slogan: "Sexuality has never been repressed" (*Politics, Philosophy, Culture*, 45). He finds the notion of repression "insidious" and admits that he can "hardly free himself of it" (*Power/Knowledge*, 119). "Why," he asks elsewhere, "do we speak with so much passion and so much resentment against our most recent past, against our present?" (*History of Sexuality*, I: 8). Foucault does not answer this question, but the answer seems obvious: The passion and resentment spring from the experience of repression and the pain that it causes.

Foucault seems to waver between two positions: (1) There is no such thing as repression, at least as he claims repression has been understood and (2) Repression is real enough but it needs to be recontextualized. We think of repression in juridical terms, on the model of law and not, more appropriately, as thoroughly modern power—diffuse, bureaucratized, and disguised. The concept rests on a series of "psychological reference points borrowed from the human sciences" (*Power/Knowledge*, 108). Here, Foucault admits that he finds it difficult to avoid Freud, as elsewhere, Marx. The principal objection to the "human sciences" as they emerged in the nineteenth century is that they are, as postmodernists like to say, "imbricated" in new forms of the exercise of power. But for Foucault, this is the case with all discourses that claim to be "true." The first claim predominates in *History of Sexuality*, Vol. I, which is the text on which I focus in this chapter.

8. Sigmund Freud, *The Freud Reader*, ed. Peter Gay (New York: W. W. Norton and Co., 1989), 742.

9. Ibid.

10. Wilhelm Reich, *Sex-Pol, Essays 1929–1934*, ed. Lee Baxandall (New York: Random House, 1972).

11. Foucault's position in many ways echoes that of the Freudo-Marxists: Capitalism "would not have been possible without the controlled insertion of bodies into the machinery of production and the adjustment of the phenomena of population to economic processes" (141). While Foucault did not believe that the economic base produces superstructural effects as its epiphenomena (a position that Reich appears to have held) he believed that mechanisms of control with varied histories and contingent causes get taken up and "colonized" by the bourgeoisie if these mechanisms further its interests (94). For

all three—Reich, Marcuse, and Foucault—mechanisms of sexual control in the modern era are closely tied to the capitalist economic order.

12. See Gad Horowitz's extremely acute comparison of Marcuse and Foucault and his compelling defense of Marcuse against Foucaultian claims. Gad Horowitz, "The Foucaultian Impasse: No Sex, No Self, No Revolution," *Political Theory* 15, no. 1 (February 1987), 61–80. For another trenchant critique of Foucault on sexuality, see Anthony Giddens, *The Transformation of Intimacy: Sexuality, Love and Eroticism in Modern Societies* (Stanford, Calif.: Stanford University Press, 1992). Giddens questions whether it is possible, as does Foucault, to write meaningfully about sexuality in the modern period, without reference to love.

13. Ladelle McWhorter, "Foucault's Attack on Sex-Desire," *Philosophy Today* (spring 1997), 160–165.

14. See Bartky, *Femininity and Domination: Studies in the Phenomenology of Oppression* (New York: Routledge), chaps. 3 and 5. See also, Susan Bordo, *Unbearable Weight* (Berkeley: University of California Press, 1993).

15. Calvin O. Schrag, *The Resources of Rationality, A Response to the Postmodern Challenge* (Bloomington: Indiana University Press, 1992), 37.

16. This is Foucault's fundamental critique of the gay rights movement. But he recognizes the impossibility of escaping from sexual specification, especially when a specific range of practices are condemned, outlawed, etc. See Foucault, *Knowledge/Power*, 220–221.

17. See Samois, ed., *What Color Is Your Handkerchief?* and *Coming to Power* (Berkeley, Calif.: Samois), 1979 and 1981, respectively. See also Linden, et al., eds., *Against Sadomasochism: A Radical Feminist Analysis* (Palo Alto, Calif.: Frog-in-the-Well Press, 1982).

18. Foucault's theoretical stance vis-à-vis the women's movement is far more positive than his response to the gay rights movement. Women, unlike gays, have made a "veritable movement of de-sexualisation, a displacement effected in relation to the sexual centering of the problem, formulating the demand for forms of culture, discourse, language, and so on, which are no longer part of that rigid assignation and pinning-down to their sex which they had initially in some sense been politically obliged to accept" (*Power/Knowledge*, 220). This has not been true of most feminist activists, and true only of poststructuralist feminist theorists who have "deconstructed" sexual difference.

Ladelle McWhorter has told me that Foucault was active in gay rights movements, and took part in gay politics; further, he was interviewed by virtually every major gay periodical in the United States and France (private communication). She asserts too that he espoused a gay identity. This seems to contradict his denial that there is a core sexual self but to recognize, as I shall shortly claim, that we have little choice but to accept, albeit provisionally, the identities foisted upon us by a misogynist and homophobic culture. "Queer theory," which began to blossom only after Foucault's death, is far closer to the poststructuralist feminism he praises than the self-understanding of the gay liberation movements that were active during his lifetime.

19. See, for example, Judith Butler, *Gender Trouble: Feminism and the Subversion of Identity* (New York: Routledge, 1990).

CHAPTER FOUR

~

Sympathy and Solidarity

I

It is by now widely conceded that feminist theories of the Second Wave (not to mention the First Wave), whatever their other virtues, have been race and class biased, heterosexist and ethnocentric, that they have often been construed as the experience of women generally, what was merely the experience of those women who, by virtue of relative race and class privilege, were in a position to theorize their experience in the first place. Disadvantaged feminists have charged relatively advantaged feminist theorists with having visited upon many of the world's women what androcentric political theory has visited upon women generally—enforced invisibility or else the distortion and falsification of the substance and texture of their lives.[1]

These charges are serious indeed in a movement that seeks to unite women across ethnic, racial, and, whenever possible, class divisions. The feminist community has tended to react to these charges in two different ways. Activists have organized workshops where, for example, white women could "work on" their racism: This "work" involves first, an unearthing of internalized racism and second, the development of greater understanding of and increased sensitivity to the lived experience of women of color. What is aimed at in such political practice is, clearly, a transformation of self—a transformation in the direction of expanded knowledge, wider sympathies and the acquisition of greater skill in the exposure and extirpation from one's psyche of submerged attitudes of superiority or condescension.

69

Feminist political theorists, on the other hand, especially those influenced by poststructuralism, have tended to regard the failure to do justice to the experience of the Other, to what is commonly called "the problem of difference," as largely a cognitive error. For feminists influenced by Derrida, the "occlusion" of difference is due to logocentrism, the mistaken belief that there is some ultimate word, presence, essence, reality, or truth that can provide a foundation for theory, experience, and expression. Such founding concepts—*logoi*—are supposed to stand outside systems of signification and guarantee their truth. But for Derrida and his followers, there are only signifying systems, systems of "difference" in which meaning is not a function of correspondence to something ultimate that stands outside the system; rather meaning is something that inheres in the differences between and among signs themselves. Further, the founding concepts of metaphysics are implicated in binary oppositions (God/world; mind/matter) in which the superior term depends covertly for its intelligibility on the inferior term which it typically denigrates or tries to ignore. The binary oppositions that ground racism, imperialism, and sexism function in just the same way and are typically linked to more familiar philosophical binaries: masculinity, for example, in a philosophical tradition that values rationality, is associated with a superior ability to reason, femininity with a denigrated intuition or emotion. As I read many postmodern texts, the critique of logocentrism and of hierarchical opposition in general construes them as cognitive: untenable metaphysical assumptions that rest on a flawed theory of meaning.[2]

Other, more empirically oriented theorists, have called for more inclusive research programs: relatively advantaged women need to learn more about the disadvantaged; they need to study the lives of others, to look and see, to ask and be instructed. Thinkers influenced by Habermas have called for the establishment of an "ideal speech situation," which would entail access for everyone to the means of interpretation and communication. While such a state of affairs could come about only after prolonged political struggle, were such a struggle to succeed, moral and political consensus, which is now manipulated by the privileged and powerful, could be built on the force of the better argument alone. Once more, the resolution of the problem of difference is conceived in largely cognitive terms.

Theorists, whatever their orientation, know that self-interest, not failure of understanding alone, often lies at the heart of the misrecognition of the Other: the solution to this disturbing insight, however, is typically posed in terms of more and better cognition. Here and there one encounters the suggestion that cognitive deficits—whether grounded in self-interest or not— are not the only things lacking in the flawed texts of contemporary feminist theory. Our capacity to enter imaginatively into the lives of others—their joys and sorrows, the peculiar texture of their suffering—is also limited. Elizabeth Spelman, in her splendid and essential *Inessential Woman*, has this to say about imagination as a corrective to bias:

> I must try to enter imaginatively into the worlds of others. Imagination isn't enough, but it is necessary. Indeed, it is a crucial starting point: because I have not experienced what the other has, so unless I can imagine her having pain or her having pleasure I can't be moved to try to help put an end to her pain or to understand what her pleasures are. Against the odds I must try to think and feel my way into her world. (Spelman 1989, 179)

Having said this, however, Spelman does an immediate about-face; imagination becomes an enticement, a snare. Imagining who the Other is, she says, is much easier than "apprenticing" oneself to the Other. Apprenticeship is demanding:

> While I am perceiving someone, I must be prepared to receive new information all the time, to adapt my actions accordingly, and to have my feelings develop in response to what the person is doing, whether I like what she is doing or not. When simply imagining her, I can escape from the demands her reality puts on me and instead construct her in my mind in such a way that I can possess her, make her into someone or something who never talks back. (Spelman 1989, 181)

In feminist theory, then, a measure of consensus has developed around the idea that the proper means to overcome bias is cognitive in nature: we must learn to identify false beliefs, for example, the belief that gender oppression can be fully understood in isolation from the oppressions of race and class (Spelman 1989, 176). We are to avoid overgeneralization, develop adequate research programs, and abandon assumptions flawed by ethnocentrism, logocentrism, binary thinking, or plain self-interest.

Now all of this is very important indeed, but it cannot be the whole story. When, after the Clarence Thomas hearings, women went around saying to each other "Men just don't get it," we were demanding more from men than the mere acquisition of knowledge. Similarly, when feminists of color take white feminists to task for racial bias, I take them to mean more than that white feminists acquire additional information or that they abandon assumptions that once seemed self-evident. What they are demanding from white women and what women, in particular feminists, demand from many men, I venture, is a knowing that transforms the self who knows, a knowing that brings into being new sympathies, new affects as well as new cognitions and new forms of intersubjectivity. The demand, in a word, is for a knowing that has a particular affective taste. But what taste is this?

Now few feminist theorists assume that knowledge and feeling are as distinct as my discussion to this point has suggested. Many philosophers have argued, quite correctly, that knowledge and feeling cannot, in all cases, be construed as conceptually distinct.[3] Certainly, particular feelings—outrage, indignation, sympathy, perhaps "empathy"—fuel the search for a more adequate knowledge of the Other; moreover, they give shape and form to this knowledge. But in my view, few theorists have examined closely enough the emotional dimension that is part of the search for better cognitions or the affective taste of the kinds of intersubjectivity that can build political solidarities.

What is it, exactly, to become more "sensitive" to the Other, in addition, that is, to my learning more about her circumstances? Does it require that I feel what she feels? Is this possible? Is it desirable? Does it require that I somehow "share" her emotion *without* feeling precisely what she feels? What is it to share an emotion with someone anyhow? Does an understanding of someone else's feelings require that I "identify" with her? If yes, what exactly is "identification"? Does a heightened sensitivity require an imaginative entry into the affective life of the Other? Again, what would such an entry be like? Is such an entry really possible? Might it have the dire consequences Spelman predicts? Does greater sensitivity require perhaps a merging of self and other? But what would merger mean in such a context and again, is such a merger possible? If it were possible, would it be desirable?

These questions call other, related questions to mind, questions that for reasons of space I shall mostly merely pose; a few I consider only briefly in the body of the chapter. Is a special affective repertoire necessary for the building of solidarities across lines of race and class that is not necessary when these lines are not crossed? We assume that the advantaged have a special obligation not only to know—in a narrow sense of "know"—but to cultivate in themselves certain affective states vis-à-vis the disadvantaged. Is it in the interest of the disadvantaged that they do likewise? Or, as some have maintained, do the disadvantaged know already all they need to know about those whose "moral luck" has cast them into more privileged social locations? Do I decide first on some purely theoretical basis who my coalition partners are to be and then somehow generate toward them the appropriate emotions? Or, since the kind of politics I am considering—feminist politics—bears an important relationship to human suffering in some, if not in all ways, does my emotional response to the suffering of others first select those others with whom I wish to be in solidarity? If I am right about the relationship between politics and suffering, and if, as is likely, everyone suffers, on what basis can

I offer myself to some sufferings and deny myself to others? And given the pervasiveness of suffering and the multitude of forms such suffering may take, how can I keep myself from getting so spent emotionally that I burn out and so turn out to be useless as a political agent? In what follows, I shall not dismiss the call, current in much feminist theory, for a better, even a radically other cognitive stance toward the Other. But instead of pursuing lines of inquiry laid out by theorists, I shall follow instead the lead of activists, whose activism has been directed to the project of self-transformation, hence to the growth and refinement of our affective repertoire.[4]

II

Phenomenologists have made the terms *Mitwelt* (shared world) and *Mitsein* (being-with) familiar to students of continental philosophy; less well known is the concept of *Mitgefühl*—literally, feeling-with. The only canonical figure in European phenomenology to have offered an extended analysis of *Mitgefühl* is Max Scheler's *Zur Phänomenologie und Theorie der Sympathiegefuhle und vom Liebe und Hass* (*The Nature of Sympathy*). In frustration at what I take to be the excessive intellectualism of much contemporary feminist theory, I turned back to the grand tradition of European phenomenology. Are there resources for feminist theory in this tradition?

The English term "sympathy" and the German "*Sympathie*" are not synonymous. Our term "sympathy" has undergone crass commercialization, as in the saccharine Hallmark "sympathy" card; moreover, there are echoes of condescension in our term that Scheler hears not so much in *Sympathie* as in the German "*Mitleid*" (pity or compassion): "A heightened commiseration bestowed from above and from a standpoint of superior power and dignity" (Scheler 1970, 40). Since it is precisely the superior power that the more advantaged feminist wishes to suspend in her intersubjective encounter with the Other, she is well-advised to avoid terms like "pity," "sympathy," or "compassion"—though compassion seems less objectionable. Scheler is more likely to use the term "*Mitgefühl*" than "*Sympathie*," but here again, there is no precise English equivalent. Scheler's translator renders "*Mitgefühl*" as "fellow-feeling," a good enough term, though slightly ludicrous in a discourse that seeks to interrogate relationships among women. In lieu of anything better and considering the fact that I was once myself a Bunting Institute "fellow," in what follows I shall use this term, also the very literal "feeling-with" and sometimes the German "*Sympathie*."

For Scheler, there are four kinds of fellow-feeling: one "true," two relatively base and lacking in moral worth and one "genuine." Scheler's conditions for "true" fellow-feeling are extremely narrow. "Two parents stand beside the dead body of a beloved child. They feel in common the 'same' sorrow, the same anguish . . . they feel it together, in the sense that they feel and experience in common" (Scheler 1970, 12). A friend who enters the room may commiserate with the parents' grief, but her feeling will not, indeed cannot, be identical to their feeling because her relationship to the child is not the same. Hence, "true" fellow-feeling is feeling identically and at the same moment what the Other is feeling, this by virtue of the fact that both feelings have the same cause. The eminent Scheler scholar, Manfred Frings, has this to say of "true" fellow-feeling: "This experience is ultimate and immediate in that the other's feeling or sorrow *is* one's own and vice-versa, so that there is no object relation to the other's feeling. Both parents are a unified subject of an irreducible, unifying sorrow" (Frings 1965, 60). Scheler is not much interested in the epistemology of the situation, whether, for example, one parent can ever know for certain whether the other is feeling precisely what she is feeling; he might, after all, be pretending. Scheler's aim is to describe immediate affective givens in situations of intersubjectivity, not to ponder abstract skeptical doubts that might later arise.

For our purposes, there is little to be learned from Scheler's "highest" form of feeling-with. The gulf between the advantaged and the disadvantaged is due in part to the fact that the causes of the misery of the one are often absent from the lives of the other. There are, of course, those who renounce their privilege by trying to produce in their own lives the conditions that cause the suffering of others. Simone Weil, for example, is said to have starved herself to death during the Second World War in order to share the sufferings of its victims. While she is a moral heroine to many, Weil's self-inflicted sufferings seem to me to have been futile, if not masochistic. To stand in solidarity with others is to work actively to eliminate their misery, not to arrange one's life so as to share it.[5]

A second form of fellow-feeling, one without moral value for Scheler, he calls "emotional infection" ("*Gefühlsansteckung*"). This occurs, for example, when I am infected by gaiety (even though I may have been depressed beforehand) upon attending a party at which others are gay and laughing. I can also be infected with the grief of others at the funeral of someone I knew only very slightly. Characteristic of "infection is the absence either of a conscious directing of one's feeling upon the Other as well as the absence of any effective knowledge of the causes of the Other's feeling" (Scheler 1970, 15). Through a process of reciprocal effect, emotional infection may gather momentum "like an avalanche," issuing in mass excitement or even a mob psychology that is "so easily carried beyond the intentions of every one of its members and does things for which no one acknowledges either the will or the responsibility" (Scheler 1970, 16). According to Frings, what Scheler has in mind are "panics, revolutions, revolts, demonstrations, strikes, etc." (Frings 1965, 62). The case against mass emotion rests on an alleged domination of more primitive drives (survival, perhaps of the herd-excitement in animals), a decrease in the level of collective intelligence, readiness for submission to a charismatic leader and, as mentioned above, an eclipse of personal responsibility. "Man becomes more of an animal by associating himself with the crowd and more of a man by cultivating his spiritual independence" (Scheler 1970, 35).

Though written well before the rise of Nazism, it is difficult not to read into this text a premonition of the fate that was to befall Scheler's Germany. Nevertheless, this is a deeply conservative position and finally, an indefensible one. Both the value ascriptions and ontological assumptions that ground Scheler's critique are questionable. Scheler places the highest value on the uniqueness and irreplaceability of the single individual; hence, the highest forms of intersubjectivity involve the sharing of emotion by two individuals or, as we shall see shortly, the intuitive apprehension of the feeling-state of one such individual by another. In emotional infection, the uniqueness of the Other never comes into play.

Scheler is one of a long line of European philosophers, stretching from Kierkegaard at least to Heidegger, who see in many social forms called forth by industrialization and urbanization nothing but a threat to the survival of individuality. A powerful counter case has been made, however, that certain of these forms, e.g., the lesbian and gay communities that first sprang up in large urban centers, both shielded and encouraged the emergence of new forms of individuality. At any rate, one can value the uniqueness and value of individuality without insisting that we must persist in retaining our sense of ourselves as discrete individuals at all times and in all places.[6] The subsumption of ourselves into a collective experience may free us temporarily from the prison-house of personality—from excessive self-absorption or stagnant self-obsession. Moreover, the assimilation of certain forms of collective action—revolts, demonstrations, and strikes—to the worst excesses of mob rule seems entirely unwarranted. Allowing for the fact that we are often unable to foresee the consequences of what we do, all other things being equal, the moral worth of collective action is a function of its specific ends and of the means employed to realize these ends. The immersion of the self in collective life, renewed periodically by an emotional "infection" that sustains such immersion, may give us the courage to develop or to express aspects of ourselves that were heretofore submerged; in this way, emotional infection may encourage not the extinction but the development of individuality.

Scheler's charges against emotional infection are misdirected not only because he overestimates the dangers of mass excitement to individual integrity, but because he seriously misdescribes the phenomenon in question. Consider the political demonstration as a paradigm case of reciprocal action "mass-excitement." We go to demonstrations not only to get a point across to those against whom we demonstrate but precisely to allow ourselves to be emotionally "infected" by one another. What infects us with the joy we feel at a good demonstration is a heightened sense of the sanity and rightness of our cause, this against the seductive "common sense" of those who stayed at home. Common sense, the sense of the "herd" that Scheler so fears, rarely needs to demonstrate. Even though we may be in the minority nationally, we, who usually feel so powerless, are infected by a sense of power emanating from the human mass we make together; moreover, the physical presence of each pledges silently to the others our continued support; in this way, we reduce our fear of isolation and defeat. We may infect each other with utopian dreams as well, the dream of "a new heaven and a new earth." While the political aims of our demonstration may, in this conservative period, be quite modest, the visionary dimension that is so much a part of the women's movement greatly exceeds such modesty; perhaps the only way a utopian vision can be kept alive and made palpable now is precisely through periodic "emotional infection." When we chant or sing together the emotional infection Scheler condemns threatens to turn into the immediate community of feeling—"true fellow feeling"—he lauds. Emotional infection as a builder of solidarity is promiscuous: its utility rests precisely in its capacity to unite in feeling persons from a very wide spectrum of social locations.

"Emotional identification" is a third form of sympathy. There are two ways in which such identification can come about: I can feel-with the other to such an extent that my self disappears entirely into her self or else I can take her ego wholly into my own (Frings 1965, 62–64). Both forms are thus extreme limiting cases of psychic infection or contagion in that in neither form does individual consciousness remain intact. "Primitive" peoples, says Scheler, are prone to such loss of self when they identify themselves with animals or ancestors. Identification can occur in dreams, hypnosis, schizophrenia, in the bond between a mother and her child, in the child playing mother to her doll when, for all intents and purposes, she becomes the mother, in states of mystic frenzy and in unvarnished sexual intercourse. Like "emotional infection," "emotional identification" lacks moral worth, this because it works directly against the development and affirmation of "deep" subjectivity, i.e., the unique individuality Scheler so values. Nell Noddings' description of care in *Caring: A Feminine Approach to Ethics and Moral Educa-*

tion would flunk Scheler's test. Here is Noddings: "I set aside my temptation to analyze and to plan. I do not project; I receive the other into myself and I see and feel with the other" (Noddings 1984, 14, 30).

We come at last to the fourth and last form of *Sympathie*: "genuine" fellow-feeling. These feelings are intentional, i.e., they have objects, indeed objects of understanding. Unlike "community of feeling," the feeling states of others are here given directly and immediately as "intentional objects" in the outward manifestations of emotion. The otherness of the Other is maintained throughout the act of genuine feeling-with; in this way, the genuine article is distinguished from contagion or identification. "For sympathy [i.e., "genuine" sympathy] presupposes that awareness of distance between selves which is eliminated by identification" (Scheler 1970, 23).[7] Further, fellow-feeling proper

> presents itself in the very phenomenon as a re-action to the state and value of the other's feelings—as these are "visualized" in vicarious feeling . . . the two functions of vicariously visualized feeling and participation in feeling are separately given and must be sharply distinguished. (Scheler 1970, 13)

I shall return later to the somewhat problematic notion of "vicarious visualization"; suffice it to say that in this passage, Scheler is trying to underscore the distinction in feeling between the one who feels and the one who feels-with.

Scheler takes violent issue with those thinkers who claim that *Sympathie* is grounded in some kind of comparison of my feelings or feeling-memories with the Other's feelings, which feelings of mine I then project into or onto the Other. On this view, I can understand and participate in your feelings only insofar as they correspond with feelings, bits of feeling or starts of feeling I have had myself. Here, Scheler takes on Theodor Lipps, whose name for this process of identification, comparison, and projection is "empathy."[8] As Scheler reads Lipps, genuine fellow-feeling begins from a question I ask myself: "How would it be if this had happened to *me*?" (Scheler 1970, 39). Scheler attacks Lipps with great ferocity: he offers a number of arguments in an attempt to rebut the empathy or what he (Scheler) sometimes calls the "genetic" theory.

First, the genetic theory is said to be ontologically unsound, holding dogmatically to a theory of human nature such that the person is a natural egoist; on such a view, fellow-feeling is indeed and can be nothing but a "*consequence* or *counterpart* of some kind to the self-regarding sentiments and attitudes" (Scheler 1970, 40). Second, the theory is said to be phenomenologically unsound. We will remember from Scheler's discussion of "emotional infection" that knowledge of the Other's circumstances forms a necessary background for a genuine *Mitgefühl*. When this condition is satisfied (together with certain other conditions which will be examined below) the Other's feeling is just *given* to me as an intentional object; I do not find in the immediacy of this "given-ness" any of the psychic processes that are supposed to ground the fellow-feeling that allows me to commiserate with the Other's misery or take joy in her joy, e.g., the sorting through of my experiences, the selection of appropriate emotion-memories, the projection into another of these memories, etc.:

> In true fellow-feeling there is no reference to the state of one's own feelings. . . . In commiserating with B, the latter's state of mind is given as located entirely in B himself; it does not filter across into A, the commiserator, nor does it produce a cor-responding or similar condition in A. It is merely "commiserated with," not under-gone by A as a real experience. (Scheler 1970, 41)

The genetic theory, so Scheler claims, is morally unsound as well.

> If in commiseration or rejoicing, we could do so only under the momentary im-pression, or illusion even, of undergoing the process *ourselves*, our attitudes would indeed appear, phenomenologically speaking, to be directed merely upon our own sorrow or joy and would therefore be an *egoistic* one. (Scheler 1970, 42)

If all I felt in apprehending your suffering was in some important way merely a rehearsal of my own suffering, I would direct my attention away from you entirely and toward the amelioration of my own misery; but this isn't what happens in genuine fellow-feeling nor is it what should happen. The moral worth of feeling-with, for Scheler, lies in its value for love. Love, in the broadest sense, is one primordial disposition of the person toward experience *per se*, more specifically, toward the *appearance* of higher values in what is ex-perienced and in the *possibility* of their realization. Egoistic rediscovery of my-self in the Other gives me no appreciation of the Other's uniqueness as a per-sonality, hence, of the Other's value-possibilities, this, for Scheler, is a necessary condition for the emergence of human love. A loving orientation toward the Other is at the basis of my desire to feel-with her; without this orientation, I would apprehend the intentional object which is the Other's emotion in a spirit of detachment or, what is worse, in a spirit of cruelty; in such a spirit, I might even take pleasure in my "vicarious visualization" of the Other's misery. There is circularity here, but it is not, I think vicious: the search for value-possibility, the loving orientation, fuels my desire for a beneficent *Mitgefühl: Mitgefühl*, in turn, can become the occasion for a cen-tered and specific love for just *this* specific individual.

Finally, Lipps' "genetic" account is flawed in that it is unable to explain how we can grow morally and spiritually in the act of encountering the Other. This theory "does nothing to account for positive unalloyed fellow-feeling which is a genuine *out-reaching* and entry into the other person and his individual situation, a true and authentic *transcendence* of one's self" (Scheler 1970, 46). Empathy theories, for Scheler, turn intersubjectivity into something akin to intrasubjectivity; they "entail that our fellow-feeling must necessarily be confined to processes and incidents in other people's experience such *as we have already met with in ourselves*" (Scheler 1970, 47). We would be incapable of any enlargement of self in its explorations of intersubjectivity if fellow-feeling were a mere epiphenomenon, hovering over the Other but having its actual grounding in us.

Scheler insists that we can have a vivid experience of someone else's joys and sorrows—even when these are merely narrated by a third party—without our having had such experiences ourselves. "My commiseration and *his* suffering are phenomenologically *two different facts*, not *one* fact . . . a person who has never felt mortal terror can still understand and envisage it just as he can also share in it" (Scheler 1970, 13, 47). Again, speaking of Jesus' despair in the Garden of Gethsemane, Scheler insists that "for every candid heart which steeps itself in that desolation, it operates not as a reminder or revival of personal sufferings, great or small, but as the revelation of a new and greater suffering hitherto undreamed of" (Scheler 1970).

III

"Genuine" fellow-feeling: how adequate an account has Scheler given us of what we can and cannot achieve in the domain of "genuine" shared emotion? There is much in Scheler's account of *Sympathie* that will interest feminists struggling with the problem of difference. I find attractive Scheler's idea that what motivates the effort to establish a positive affective bond with the Other is love. "Love" is not precisely the term we need: perhaps "solidarity" or even "sisterhood" or a strong disposition toward sisterhood or solidarity would serve our purposes better. Feminist theory is mistaken in having elevated cognition over this affective dimension that, whatever it is, is somehow akin to love. Second Wave feminists were wrong or even arrogant in having believed that we had already achieved sisterhood, but we were surely wrong too in allowing ourselves to be shamed for having committed ourselves to it at all. Finally, then, it is an effect—something akin to love or to the yearning for a more solidary world in which one might love others and be loved by them in return—that sounds consistently, like an organ-point, under the multifarious attempts to reduce the cognitive deficits in our understanding of the Other.

Theories of normative intersubjectivity that rely too heavily on cognition are unbalanced, but theories that give it too little weight are flawed as well. Scheler's emphasis on knowledge of the Other's circumstances as a necessary precondition for genuine fellow-feeling echoes nicely Spelman's idea of an "apprenticeship" of the more advantaged to the less advantaged. It is precisely the lack—or putative lack—of an adequate knowledge of the Other that motivates Scheler's attack both on emotional infection and emotional identification. Valuable too in Scheler's account is his emphasis on the ineradicable otherness of the Other, as well as his uncompromising insistence that "genuine" fellow-feeling must provide an occasion for moral and, I would add, political development.

The otherness of the Other: What does this mean? Some feminists might find Scheler's insistence on the maintenance of ego-boundaries in cases of genuine fellow-feeling excessively masculinist. Furthermore, as I argued earlier, the loss of a sense of oneself as a distinct self in the experience of merger with a collective subject as happens, e.g., in political demonstrations, can be a powerful impetus to the building of solidarities. Now while such experiences can be a source of political bonding, they are fleeting. When the parade is over, the disadvantaged stands before the one advantaged in her stigmatized and despised social identity; the one advantaged faces the Other secure, say, in her enjoyment of heterosexual privilege or in her "shameful livery of white incomprehension" (Bulhan 1985, 122). To maintain a sense of separateness even within a profound experience of feeling-with can be a powerful deterrent to the dangers inherent in such a situation. The ineradicable distance between persons can act against the temptation on the part of the one disadvantaged—if she finds profound commiseration and understanding in the one advantaged—to try to overleap and deny her oppressed condition in an act of emotional merger. It can discourage the temptation on the part of the advantaged one to believe that her oppressor's guilt can be overcome through heroic acts of ego-identification. The emphasis on the non-identity of the feeling of the one who feels and the feeling of the one who feels-with works against the tendency on the part of the advantaged, through a priori constructions of all kinds, to rob the disadvantaged of her specificity and uniqueness: the preservation of the otherness of the Other works against her re-colonization.

Finally, Scheler's emphasis on the necessity of some emotional distance in acts of *Sympathie* may shed light on a problem posed earlier, which I shall call the "wretchedness" problem: insofar as political activists are fully cognizant of and emotionally attuned to the wretchedness of the wretched of the earth, how can we save ourselves from despair, or from a psychological paralysis that could rob us of political effect? The relatively advantaged in the developed world are for the most part culpably indifferent to the miseries of most of the rest of the world as well as of the less fortunate in their own societies. Many blame victims for their victimization. Most lead excessively privatized lives that lack any effective or persistent sense of political outrage: the retreat into private life is quite consonant with the highly convenient belief that "you can't change the system." But for those sufficiently advantaged to have a choice, it is difficult to steer a course between privatization on the one hand and despair at the vastness of human misery on the other. Perhaps Scheler's distinction between feeling and feeling-with hints at a solution. We do not share the sufferings of those with whom we want to stand in solidarity. Their suffering is the intentional object to which our commiseration, a "vicarious visualization" is directed. While there are points of similarity between a feeling and that feeling commiserated-with (as my discussion below will indicate), nonetheless, *the two are not identical.* I commiserate with your sufferings and take joy in your joys (how odd that we have no verb for this in English!) but I experience neither your suffering nor your joy; they are *yours.* Perhaps the wretchedness problem arises because we fear that were we to open ourselves fully to the miseries of others, we would be plunged headlong into the very depths of this misery. Scheler's cautionary phenomenology of "genuine" feeling-with assures us that this need not happen.

IV

Though I find Scheler's account of authentic *Sympathie* highly suggestive for the construction of a political phenomenology of solidarity, as I shall argue below, I find it exceedingly impressionistic and in important ways, incomplete. *Sympathie*, for Scheler, consists in this: the immediate, intuitive apprehension of the Other's feeling given to me *as* "vicariously visualized" by myself. Now, the first part of this, the idea of "immediate apprehension" seems to me plausible. Understood, of course, is the existence of a complex set of background circumstances which surround this givenness: e.g., linguistic competence sufficient to know what to call what is given, knowledge of the sorts of circumstances that produce the given as well as its behavioral manifestations in my culture or, as the case may be, in other cultures. "Vicarious visualization" is far more problematic; I shall return to it later.

The idea of "immediate apprehension" is Scheler's way of insisting that I need not experience an emotion first *myself* in order to recognize what it is. Like the American pragmatist, George Herbert Mead, Scheler maintains that knowledge of self does not precede the knowledge of others. Originally,

> The child feels the feelings and thinks the thoughts of those who form his social environment, and there is one broad roaring stream of living in which he is totally immersed. It takes a long time before vortices form within this stream, which draw together what later on will clearly be recognized as "mine" and "other." (Stark, in Scheler 1970, xxxix)

There is of course some question whether the emotional capacities of children are still present, at least incipiently, in adults. But to deny that they are is to maintain the depressing view that our emotional repertoire is established in childhood and is never again subject to significant expansion. Moreover, the idea that I cannot understand what you are feeling unless I have felt something similar myself recalls the odd notion of *anamnesis*, i.e., the idea that I can never learn anything new, only remember what it was I already knew. We would not want to claim that it is *anamnesis* that makes possible our knowledge of physical objects or of mathematical signs, why then our understanding of other people's emotions?

Scheler's phenomenology is addressed to the following sort of question: How can I understand, on some level at least, the horror of the Holocaust without having been a Holocaust victim myself? As I read Scheler, he maintains that this sense of horror appears, phenomenologically speaking, not to have been put together out of bits and pieces of my own experience but to arise from my capacity to intuit the feeling states and experiences of others. I do not construct the phenomenon out of my own affective materials: I grasp it, not inferentially but intuitively, "immediately." Nor is there anything incorrigible about immediate apprehension: Such apprehensions do not guarantee that I always get things right. We must remember that Scheler's primary concern is to offer a descriptive phenomenology of *Mitgefühl*, not to resolve questions concerning its veracity. At any rate, the skeptical doubts that we might raise about the reliability of my fellow-feelings can be brought against Lipps' "genetic theory" as well.

The idea of comparison as the primary structure of *Mitgefühl* Scheler associates with an essentially self-regarding view of the person, the idea of intuition with the notion that we have important other-regarding capacities. I do not ascribe to Scheler the denial that we *ever* infer what others are feeling, only the claim that inference is not the paradigmatic core of *Mitgefühl*. Nor does the "immediacy" of *Sympathie* mean that no mediation is required to narrow the distance between myself and the Other: as noted earlier, substantial background information is often needed, as well as linguistic competence, ordinary emotional capacities, etc. What is "immediate" here, I venture, is the idea that once the proper background conditions are satisfied, I can "leap" out of my own experience into an intuitive understanding of the Other's emotional life. This leap from the "I" to the "Thou" is not a merger with the "Thou" nor is it a comparison between an "I" and a "Thou" which would be little more than a reconstructed "I." Lipps' genetic theory does not account as well for the transformative character of Scheler's *Mitgefühl*: The barriers that ordinarily separate selves fall and I behold something *new*, something that may well transform my self, even the self whose state I "intuit."

Scheler never sets out clearly what he means by "vicarious visualization." "Vicarious" is defined in my dictionary as "performed or suffered in place of another," as "taking the place of another" or as "felt or enjoyed by imagining oneself to participate in the experience of others" (*Random House Dictionary* 1980, 969). Given Scheler's extended polemic against Lipps, the choice of the term "vicarious" seems singularly inapt, if not inconsistent. In spite of this and in the absence of any textual direction from Scheler, I shall now simply stipulate a meaning for the idea of "vicarious visualization" that will, I hope, flesh out Scheler's rather thin theory of *Sympathie* while preserving the core of his critique of Lipps.

I suggest that we take "vicarious visualization" to refer to imagination. No account of *Mitgefühl*, in my view, can omit imagination as a core factor in its phenomenology; nor is it necessary to reduce imagination to a function that is fundamentally self-regarding. Imagination must share triple billing with cognition and "love" in any phenomenology of *Sympathie*.

V

Earlier I cited Spelman, who rejects imagination on behalf of cognitive apprenticeship. But there are in fact two senses of imagination at work in Spelman's text: one kind of imagining is inattentive to the Other, merely constructing her "in my mind in such a way that I can possess her." Spelman's rejection of imagination of this sort echoes Scheler's claim that both "emotional identification" and empathy theory can find in fellow-feeling merely a form of egoism in disguise. But Spelman notes that there is another way to imagine, one that involves the capacity "to enter imaginatively into the worlds of others," without stretching these Others on the Procrustean bed of my own experience.

Consider in this connection the words of the Haggadah, the service for the Jewish Passover. In this text, I am told that "it is incumbent upon every Israelite in every generation to imagine if *he* (sic) has actually gone out from Egypt" (Haggadah, 29). I must imagine that I myself was oppressed with great rigor as a slave in Egypt, that with signs and portents, I myself was led out of Egypt by Jehovah with a mighty hand and an outstretched arm, etc. The question then is this: am I an egoist if I obey the instruction of the Haggadah? If I imagine myself part of that multitude, have I thereby put myself center stage? Have I usurped a place that belongs to others or have I achieved, in Scheler's words, a "genuine *out-reaching* and entry into the other person and his individual situation"?

I might of course make myself the star of the show, but I need not; I can imagine the scene from Exodus any way I like. Imagination, says Edward Casey, is the least constrained of all our faculties (Casey 1976). I can, if I wish, see myself merely as one of a terrified multitude, with the Pharoah's army at our backs and the still unparted sea before us. Or I can imagine what it would be like to be *someone*, indeed anyone, on that distant shore: that someone need not be myself. Such imagining, if it is sufficiently vivid, is surely in harmony with the spirit of the Haggadah, if not its letter. Now there is a trivial sense in which *my* imagining as *mine* always bears some reference to myself, but it does not follow from this either that my imagining of another's feeling is invariably a sign of egoism or that in such imagining I must always put myself in the picture.

Indeed, there are situations in which I can imagine the suffering of others without putting myself in the picture at all. Nawal El Saadawi, the noted Egyptian feminist, describes in *The Hidden Face of Eve* how, as a small child, she was awakened in the middle of the night by her mother and some other of her female relatives, dragged from her bed and then, without anesthesia, forced to undergo a clitoridectomy. She had not been told about the practice of clitoridectomy and was utterly unprepared for what was done to her. I can imagine this scene without in any way substituting myself, who never endured such treatment, for the small child who did.

What, one might ask, is the difference between just knowing the facts of this case—a knowledge virtually certain, at least among Western knowers, to produce a powerful emotional response—and an imaginative projection into it? While I will not try to define "imagination" *tout court*, the term naming a wide variety of mental acts, the kind of imagining to which I refer would involve specific forms of ideation, including "visualization." In this case, it seems plausible to claim that the better I can visualize the sets of circumstances that give rise to the Other's emotion, as well as the behavioral aspects of the emotion ("She screamed in terror"; "She begged for mercy") the better I can feel-with the victim. Clearly, there is a difference between a mere knowing-that, even a knowing that can list concretely and in detail the circumstances of the case and a "vicarious visualization" that causes these circumstances to come alive in the theater of my mind.

This discussion is plagued by the over-reliance in Western philosophy on metaphors of seeing: visualization, "intuition" (from the Latin "to look upon"), my own earlier "beholding," now "theater of the mind," an image that reinforces the idea of spectatorship. While the idea of an internal seeing has an important role in the conception of imagination and is certainly appropriate in the case we are considering, we ought not forget its limitations. Thus, in reading El Saadawi's text, I must, to be sure, produce an active and vivid picturing to myself of the details of the scene, a more active and vivid picturing than is necessary to grasp the bare facts of the case. I must conjure up in my "mind's eye" the dark bedroom, the shadowy figures of the adults. But here the idea of seeing must give way to something else: I may "see" the utter terror of the child, her bewilderment and sense of betrayal, but I must imagine as well what it was for her to have *felt* this terror, this absolute incomprehension in the face of the cruelty of those she trusted. I must imagine not only the sight of the knife as it cuts her flesh; I must try to imagine what she feels as it cuts her flesh. (How unfortunate that even our term "imagination" contains within it the idea of an "image"—of something seen—when much of what we must learn to imagine is not something seen at all.)

With Scheler and against Lipps, I can do this—can I not?—without putting myself in place of the child; I do not think of myself at all. Nor is my imagining really mine in any but the most trivial sense: El Saadawi's description of the scene is so vivid that to read it is to be haunted by it perhaps for the rest of one's life. She, as author of her text and authority on her memories, is stage manager and director; I am not. Nor, when I imagine myself in the Exodus, do I direct the scene either. It seems to me that I am seeing either the strange medieval wood-cuts in my parents' ancient Haggadah, or else some film.[9]

Furthermore, far from putting myself in El Saadawi's picture, I can imagine an indefinite number of small girls, past, present, and, sadly, future, who will be subjected to similar ordeals: my intentional objects have proliferated; differently put, a collective intentional object has emerged for which I have *Mitgefühl*. This points up another feature of Scheler's phenomenology that stands in need of elaboration. His model of fellow-feeling takes as paradigmatic a one-on-one relationship between, say, the one who is assaulted and the one who commiserates with the one assaulted. He has nothing to say about the experience of fellow-feeling for an entire class of persons rather than for a single individual, or of one human collective for another.

Scheler's phenomenology of *Mitgefühl* raises a host of questions it cannot answer. How can one learn to feel-with the many, not just the one? Whence comes that "love"—that deep need for solidarity—that makes us want to know the Other in all her complexity? Indeed, why are most people's sympathies so narrow? Why can they feel-with, at most, an individual stranger, a friend or two, family members, or the occasional beached whale? Why are so many of us unable to feel-with—"the wretched of the earth"? Do contemporary modes of the transmission of information deprive us systematically of the kind of context that is integral to feeling-with? Or does the fault lie perhaps in ourselves, in an underdeveloped imagination, in a willed withholding of feeling for the unfortunate, in culpable ignorance of the state and condition of millions of our fellow creatures? Is it the case, as Diana Meyers (1994) has argued, that culturally entrenched figurations of despised, different Others block feeling-with? Or are we afraid that such widespread suffering demands sacrifices of us that we are unwilling to make? Does the refusal or inability to feel-with lie perhaps in the very vastness of human suffering, in the frustration we encounter in trying to represent to ourselves what is unrepresentable? Does it lie perhaps in the anxiety that we ourselves may fall into the abyss that has claimed so many others? How can the rush of normally temporary compassion brought on by reports of some current injustice be mined for progressive political ends? One thing is clear: the effort to construct a phenomenology of feeling-with cannot go forward without the parallel construction of its opposites: feeling too little for others or feeling nothing at all. And so we walk a tightrope with Scheler: to fall to one side is to land in a state of despondency, excessive privatization or indifference; to fall the other way is to plunge into the manifold deformations of fellow-feeling, into constructions of the Other that are self-serving, phantasmatic, or condescending.

VI

Having framed this essay in terms of feminist theory, it seems appropriate to conclude with a few remarks that bear on the relationship of the foregoing discussion to political feminism. Few of the mass-based movements that took shape in the 1960s and 1970s have survived the long shift to the right that followed; of these movements, the contemporary women's movement, it seems to me, has demonstrated the most consistent commitment to the building of solidarities across lines of class, race, ethnicity, and sexual orientation. The results of this commitment have been, not surprisingly, mixed.

Postmodern feminism seems today to enjoy hegemony, at least among academic feminists. Its defenders claim that postmodernism is superior to other feminisms first, because it alone properly valorizes "difference," so often submerged and denigrated within the conventional conceptual hierarchies of totalizing Western theory and second, because it calls in radical fashion for the "deconstruction" not only of gender—the cultural meanings inscribed in biological sex—but of "sex" itself. Our ideas of "the biological" with its division into "natural kinds" is said to be no less socially constructed than other, more obvious markers of sexual difference (Butler 1990, 1993).

Postmodern feminism is, in some respects, a theoretical advance over some of the feminisms that preceded it. But, to paraphrase Marx on Hegel, it is not enough to valorize difference in thought when our movement has yet to develop a practice adequate to the real diversity among women, nor is it sufficient to "deconstruct" gender in thought when it continues to inhabit our consciousness and to structure much of our everyday life. Questions of practice, indeed *theoretical* questions about appropriate practice, have latterly been neglected in favor of "pure" theory. But between the purest of theory and the most concrete practice there lies an intermediate sphere, a sphere concerned chiefly with problems of movement-building. This sphere is quite vast; I took up residence in this essay in one corner of it, asking more questions than I answer. More attention should be paid to the theorizing of a more fruitful practice, otherwise feminist theory may well become a theory without a practice. If feminism is primarily addressed to the suffering of women, what could be more urgent?

Notes

I wish to thank Isaac Balbus in particular for his detailed critical engagement with this chapter. The following persons offered extremely helpful critical comments on earlier versions of the chapter: Lorraine Code, Charles Mills, David Schweickart, Paul Gomberg, Diana Meyers, and Nancy Frankenberry.

This chapter was previously published in *Feminists Rethink the Self*, edited by Diana Tietjens Meyers (Boulder, Colo.: Westview Press, 1997).

1. See, e.g., bell hooks, *Ain't I a Woman: Black Women and Feminism* (Boston: South End Press, 1981) and *Feminist Theory: From Margin to Center* (Boston: South End Press, 1984); Elizabeth V. Spelman, *Inessential Woman: Problems of Exclusion in Feminist Theory* (Boston: Beacon Press, 1989); Maria Lugones and Elizabeth V. Spelman, "Have We Got a Theory for You! Feminist Theory, Cultural Imperialism and the Demand for a 'Woman's Voice,'" in *Women and Values: Readings in Recent Feminist Philosophy* (Belmont, Calif.: Wadsworth, 1993).

2. For an excellent sample of Derridean and other poststructuralist approaches to feminist theory, see Judith Butler and Joan W. Scott, eds., *Feminists Theorize the Political* (New York: Routledge, 1992).

3. See, e.g., Anthony Kenny, *Action, Emotion and the Will* (London: Routledge and Kegan Paul, 1963); J. R. S. Wilson, *Emotion and Object* (Cambridge: Cambridge University Press, 1972); R. M. Gordon, "Aboutness of Emotion," *American Philosophical Quarterly* 11, no. 1 (January 1974); Robert Solomon, "The Logic of Emotion," *Nous* 11, no. 1 (1977), and *The Passions* (New York: Doubleday, 1976); Irving Thalberg, "Emotion and Thought," *American Philosophical Quarterly* 1 (1964) and *Perception, Emotion and Action* (Oxford: Basil Blackwell, 1977); Donald Davidson, "Hume's Cognitive Theory of Pride," *Journal of Philosophy* 73, no. 19 (November 1976); Gabriele Taylor, *Pride, Shame and Guilt: Emotions of Self-Assessment* (Oxford: Oxford University Press, 1985).

4. Since I write from the perspective of a relatively advantaged woman, the "Other" in this essay is relatively disadvantaged. But questions about the effects and intersubjective postures that are appropriate to the building of cross-class and cross-racial solidarities is important for the disadvantaged as well. In certain respects, then, the roles of self and Other in this essay can be reversed.

5. Sometimes, of course, the nature of one's political work *requires* sharing the hardships of the poor, the oppressed, etc., but sometimes it does not.

6. Scheler assumes here and in other writings a stable, core self, an assumption that has come under fire from postmodernists. An examination in depth of this issue would take me far afield. I shall assume, with Scheler, a self sufficiently stable enough to participate in the forms of intersubjectivity he describes.

7. I have added the material in brackets.

8. The modern use of the term "empathy" dates from 1897 when Lipps introduced the term *"Einfühlung"* in a treatise on aesthetics. There, the term refers to the tendency of the viewer to lose self-awareness and fuse with the object of aesthetic consciousness. Edward B. Titchener of Cornell first introduced the term "empathy" as an equivalent for Lipps' *"Einfühlung."* We now use the term "empathy" very broadly, even to characterize the kinds of *Sympathie* that inhabit Scheler's phenomenology. What is important to remember is that Scheler is offering a specific critique of Lipps' account of the origin and nature of *Mitgefühl*, sympathy, fellow-feeling or—if we slip into current linguistic practice—"empathy." The issue has to do with the nature of the phenomenon, not its name. (See Lipps, 1903–6, 1907–12.)

9. As the example of *The Hidden Face of Eve* illustrates, *Mitgefühl* can come about in the absence of personal connection, in this case through literature. Enlightened education, especially an aesthetic education that offered training in mimesis and sense-memory, could increase markedly our capacities for fellow-feeling. Current battles for control of U.S. education, with an organized right wing pitted against those who favor a more multicultural curriculum, should be evaluated in this context. What is at stake in this battle is control not only of the transmission of ideas but of training in the capacity for wider sympathies.

References

Bulhan, Hussein Abdilahi. 1985. *Frantz Fanon and the Psychology of Oppression*. New York: Plenum Press.

Butler, Judith. 1990. *Gender Trouble: Feminism and the Subversion of Identity*. New York: Routledge.

———. 1993. *Bodies that Matter: On the Discursive Limits of "Sex."* New York: Routledge.

Butler, Judith, and Joan W. Scott, eds. 1992. *Feminists Theorize the Political*. New York: Routledge.

Casey, Edward. 1976. *Imagining: A Phenomenological Study*. Bloomington: Indiana University Press.

Code, Lorraine. 1991. *What Can She Know? Feminist Theory and the Construction of Knowledge*. Ithaca, N.Y.: Cornell University Press.

Davidson, Donald. 1976. "Hume's Cognitive Theory of Pride." *Journal of Philosophy* 73 (19).

El Saadawi, Nawal. 1980. *The Hidden Face of Eve*. London: Zed Books.

Frings, Manfred. 1965. *Max Scheler*. Pittsburgh: Duquesne University Press.

Gordon, R. M. 1974. "Aboutness of Emotion." *American Philosophical Quarterly* 11 (1).

hooks, bell. 1981. *Ain't I a Woman: Black Women and Feminism*. Boston: South End Press.

———. 1984. *Feminist Theory: From Margin to Center*. Boston: South End Press.

Kenny, Anthony. 1963. *Action, Emotion and the Will*. London: Routledge and Kegan Paul.

Lipps, Theodor. 1885. *Psychologische Studien*. F. Vieweg u. Sohn.

———. 1903–6. *Aesthëtik*. 2 vols. B. G. Teubner Verlag.

———. 1907–12. *Psychologische Untersuchungen*. 2 vols. B. G. Teubner Verlag.

Lugones, Maria, and Elizabeth V. Spelman. 1993. "Have We Got a Theory for You! Feminist Theory, Cultural Imperialism and the Demand for the 'Woman's Voice.'" In *Women and Values: Readings in Recent Feminist Philosophy*, edited by Marilyn Pearsall. 2nd ed. Belmont, Calif.: Wadsworth.

Meyers, Diana Tietjens. 1994. *Subjection and Subjectivity: Psychoanalytic Feminism and Moral Philosophy*. New York: Routledge.

Noddings, Nell. 1984. *Caring: A Feminine Approach to Ethics and Moral Education*. Berkeley: University of California Press.

Passover Haggadah with Music. 1912. New York: Hebrew Publishing Co.

Random House Dictionary. 1980. New York: Ballantine Books.

Scheler, Max. 1970. *The Nature of Sympathy*. Peter Heath, trans. with a general introduction by W. Stark. Hamden, Conn.: Archon Books. (This work was first published in Germany in 1913.)

Solomon, Robert. 1976. *The Passions*. New York: Doubleday.

———. 1977. "The Logic of Emotion." *Nous* 11 (1).

Spelman, Elizabeth. 1989. *Inessential Woman: Problems of Exclusion in Feminist Theory*. Boston: Beacon Press.

Taylor, Gabriele. 1985. *Pride, Shame and Guilt: Emotions of Self-Assessment*. Oxford: Oxford University Press.

Thalberg, Irving. 1964. "Emotion and Thought." *American Philosophical Quarterly* 1.

Wilson, J. R. S. 1972. *Emotion and Object*. Cambridge: Cambridge University Press.

CHAPTER FIVE

~

Unplanned Obsolescence:
Some Reflections on Aging

Grow old along with me,
The best is yet to be,
The last of life for which the first was made.

—Robert Browning

What was there precisely about the "last of life" that the poet thinks is best? And how are we to understand Browning's teleology? In what sense is the first of life made for the last? The poet has fallen in love and rescued Elizabeth Barrett, much of whose youth had been spent under the thumb of a tyrannical Victorian father and in the grip of psychosomatic illness, both of which had colluded in her virtual imprisonment in the family home. But surely, these lines are meant to have a more general appeal; indeed, they are among the most quoted in English verse. These lines were quoted to me often by my father, on the occasion of anyone's birthday. My father was relentlessly cheerful, his cheerfulness barely covering a chronic mild depression. Naturally, his perpetual optimism produced in me an equal and opposite reaction: pessimism.

Unlike the poet and my father, I see old age, for the most part, as a series of mini- and maxi-disasters, largely as a series of losses, from the loss of one's social or professional networks, the loss, if one lives long enough, of one's life-companion, the loss, if one is unlucky, of motility, or sight, or hearing, or the control of one's sphincters, or all, the loss of one's home, if illness requires moving in with an adult child or else incarceration in a nursing home

("Abandon All Hope, Ye Who Enter Here"), to the ultimate loss—to death. For purposes of this essay, I follow Sara Ruddick in defining "old age," the so-called "Golden Years," as beginning at seventy. This is, of course arbitrary. Some people are stooped, played out, and washed up in their forties, while many of the "elderly" are energetic, vibrant, creative, and attractive. But the chronological stages of life are, however we see ourselves and others, a social as well as a legal fact.[1] You can't drive a car in Illinois unless you're sixteen or legally get a drink until you're twenty-one. There are inflexible age floors under Social Security and Medicare and it would be stupid not to join the AARP and let it lobby in our interest or to take advantage of all the "Senior Citizen" discounts we can get. If I were younger I might define old age as beginning at sixty-five, as does Margaret Walker. But as I write this, I am sixty-two, feeling still like an eternal undergraduate, scarcely adjusted to "middle age," much less to crossing that lonesome valley in just three more years.

I shall enumerate some of the losses that aging brings: the list is not intended to be comprehensive and it is strongly influenced by what I myself fear. I write as a white, middle-class professional with a secure income, health insurance, and the prospect of a pension I can live on comfortably. My situation thus protects me against two great evils, racism and poverty, whose effects fall even more heavily on a vulnerable population such as the elderly. Nor do I have aging parents or adult children or grandchildren for whom I must care. I am childless and my parents are dead. Where I see gains accruing to the elderly, I will mention them. When this exercise has been completed, I shall put my entire narrative, as the Derrideans say, "under erasure," in order to try to determine which of these losses are the consequence of ideological manipulation, the inability to imagine alternatives to standard scripts, "socially constructed" (hence in principle alterable) and which are irremediable features of the human condition.

I. The Loss of Social and Professional Networks

As we age, our friends die and our social circle shrinks; this is part of the loneliness and isolation that beset older people. While it is important to figure out how to make new friends, the old friends, with whom I bonded in some cases for over forty years, are not so easily replaced. It was easier to make friends when I was younger and relatively unformed. Now I know what I believe, what are my values, commitments, and politics. What my generation has seen, the history of which we were a part, is part of who I am as well. Few people will understand these things for they were not part of them. It is unlikely that I will encounter in the lady next door or in the supermarket line someone who will. I find it virtually impossible to convey to my young students what it was like to have lived through a period of significant social ferment. While it is important for the generations to speak together, I need as intimates people of my generation who remember *what it was like*—not just the cataclysmic events, e.g., the assassination of Martin Luther King Jr., but the flavor and texture of the vanished popular culture of our youth. This is why I react very negatively to the suggestion that age-segregated housing be outlawed. There is a very great pleasure and comfort in being with one's own generation that militates somewhat against the loss through death of close friends.

Complaint as well as reminiscence gives comfort: the elderly need to be able to complain to one another about things that younger people cannot understand or would be bored to hear about. I don't see that this is incompatible with being active and effective in the world for I can find out what younger people are thinking and doing without having to live with them. The elderly ought to have some choice in the matter of housing. I have no obligation to maintain a facade of friendliness with neighbors with whom I have nothing in common nor do I have an obligation either to be interested in other people's children or to put up with their noise.

Many of us have been active in organizing and sustaining professional networks. These networks accomplished a great deal. One of the most successful examples of professional networking was the organization of the Gay and Lesbian Caucus of the American Psychological Association. This organization succeeded in having homosexuality removed from the standard reference list of psychological abnormalities; they changed the ontology of their field.[2] Female professionals in the APA continue to struggle against the inclusion of categories that will harm women by classifying as a matter of individual pathology patterns that are the result of patriarchal social relations, e.g., "masochistic personality disorder."

The Society for Women in Philosophy exposed sexism in job interviews and in academic employment generally, helped to launch feminist philosophy as a more or less respectable field in philosophy, carried on profound critiques of all manner of philosophical traditions, demanded inclusion on editorial boards and on committees, got the American Philosophical Association to put out a newsletter on feminism and philosophy, and started a successful journal, *Hypatia*. We were, I know, a factor in the belated but critical organizing of the Gay and Lesbian Philosophical Society. We got feminist philosophy onto the regular program, made common cause and planned joint programs with other groupings within the larger organization, e.g., the Committee on Blacks in Philosophy and the Radical Philosophy Association. In a word, we had an impact. But even successful organizations like this, have, like people, a life cycle. While what happens is not the same for every group, over time, often the "founding mothers" die or retire; the organization disappears or changes its focus; younger women appear who wish to take the organization in directions its founders may not have approved. The old militancy appears to vanish before the problems against which it militated have been resolved. New groupings of women appear, some fairly conservative, who do not share the more radical vision of the founding cohort: sometimes the opposite happens. The older aims and strategies, indeed, the older vision has become obsolete.

I have seen creeping obsolescence happen to older men in the APA; formerly influential, both philosophically and professionally. Their comrades die or retire; they lose whatever influence they once had; they appear lost and stranded, polar bears on an ice floe. I watched this happen to my own dissertation advisor. The Whiteheadian and neopragmatist orientation of his generation gave way completely to linguistic analysis and the new positivism: he died shortly after retirement. His work was influential in its day; few read him now.

There are, of course, networks that are somewhat more formal than loose affiliations of friends and that are not organized around wage work. My Aunt Lil, my mother's only sister and her best friend, belonged to such a group, the Wednesday Club. "The Wednesday girls," as they always called themselves, met weekly for almost forty years. There were eight or nine of them, close friends all, who shared each other's joys and sorrows for most of their lives. Their names were household words to me because even though my mother (much younger than my aunt) was not a Wednesday girl herself, she knew them all. Aunt Lilly and my mother spent hours every day on the telephone; the struggles and sorrows, the small victories and defeats of the Wednesday girls were discussed in detail. This talk was background to my play. My father teased my mother for spending so much time on the telephone; he had no idea what it was like for a vital and energetic person like my mother to be held captive in her home by the demands of childcare. My aunt's daughters were in high school, but she lived too far away to walk and she didn't drive.

The Wednesday girls were daughters of immigrants. None had been to college, nor had their husbands. Most of the husbands were salesmen or small businessmen who managed to make enough money to keep their wives out of wage work (a marker in those days of arrival in the middle class) though some of the women "helped out" in the family business, indeed, probably helped run it. But Wednesday afternoons were sacrosanct. I went one time at my aunt's invitation to a Wednesday gathering. This must have been someone's birthday or anniversary and Aunt Lilly wanted to make the afternoon a bit special. So she hired me, the family piano prodigy, to play Chopin quietly in the background while she served petit fours, finger sandwiches, and tea. Of course the Wednesday girls made a terrific fuss over me: how pretty I was, how talented! They dressed for each other, in fashionable frocks or chic suits with padded shoulders and handsome Bakelite buttons. (They all sewed, and well.) They wore funny little hats. They were, by the standards of the day, slim. Their long fingernails were blood red, their hairdos à la mode, their shoes two-toned leather with open toes. After lunch and a lot of talking, these elegant ladies settled happily into their games of mah jong. Over the years, everything was shared—the success of a child, the failure of a business. What astonishes me now about the Wednesday girls is the readiness and effectiveness of their emotional and material support of one another, the surprising cohesiveness of the group and its longevity. I believe that in some important sense, the Wednesday girls loved each other.

Of course, they aged. Their husbands grew ill, mostly with heart conditions. It was thought better for the husbands if they retired and moved south, mostly to Florida or Arizona. Or was it thought better *by* the husbands to move south where one could play golf year round? I wonder how many of these women really wanted to uproot themselves. Then the husbands began to die. The Wednesday girls gave immense comfort and support to one another on these occasions. But as no one in the club was very rich and because they had no pensions in their own name, many of the Wednesday girls found that they could not live on what their husbands had left them. So, increasingly, they moved in with adult children, rarely a happy arrangement. And the children were scattered, many to California. So little by little, the fabric of the Wednesday club was rent and then, one day, it unraveled; it was no more. They kept in touch with one another, to be sure, but the news from points South was never very good. As these lifelong friends of my aunt had become lifelong friends of my mother too, I sometimes saw them when they made brief stopovers in Chicago to see friends or family still in the North. As older women, they had lost their verve and chic; they looked dowdy, thicker, gray of face, defeated.

Networks are born, mature, sustain us and our projects and then almost certainly decline. We have drawn sustenance from these networks, sometimes even a part of our identity and certainly self-esteem. When they disappear we sustain losses, sometimes profound losses; the image of the ice floe returns.

II. The Loss of an Effective Political Vision

While this is by no means universal, most people having little, if any, political vision, it is not uncommon. Our political hopes and activisms, like our professional and social networks, have been for many, a virtual lifelong commitment, a significant source of value and meaning, identity, and self-worth. Consider, for example, those environmentalists who see the world environment steadily deteriorating; the political address to these issues is so slight (and in many places nonexistent) that these activists must feel like Cassandra of Troy: they prophesy disaster but no one is listening. No one today shares the belief that sustained so many dissidents during much of the last two hundred years, i.e., that "history is on our side."

An extended example: consider the experience of Charlotte Perkins Gilman and of her generation of feminists. Gilman devoted most of her adult life to the women's movement: she was an effective lecturer, a journalist who edited a successful and influential progressive periodical, a novelist, an economist, an able and provocative feminist theoretician, highly critical of the family, of housing arrangements, and of the organization of domestic labor. She was part of the generation of feminists who had agitated most of their adult lives for the suffrage, and who lived to see, finally, the enactment of the Nineteenth Amendment. Like many feminist leaders of her generation, she believed that once women got the vote they would enact sweeping reforms that would clear the way for a society of social justice. But no such thing happened. What happened instead was the election of the corrupt and incompetent Warren Harding and then of the totally lackluster Calvin Coolidge. The country took a sharp turn to the right: the Klan grew rapidly in Indiana and in many northern states. The progressive and socialist movements that had invigorated political life before the First World War were in eclipse. The younger women to whom feminists of Gilman's generation assumed they would pass the torch appeared not to want it. What many wanted instead was a release from what they saw as Victorian prudery: instead of sweeping the country free of backward institutions and corrupt politicians, they altered but did not challenge the institutions of heterosexuality. Skirts went from the floor to the knee and above: there were bold public displays of body parts that had been covered for aeons. The bathing beauty contest was invented in Atlantic City from whence it spread. (Ironically, the first public demonstration of Second Wave feminism was held during the Miss America contest—in Atlantic City.) Young women wore makeup, shaved their legs, bobbed their hair, demanded the right to date, unchaperoned. The ubiquity of the automobile created private spaces that had not existed before.

Now Gilman was indeed Victorian in her sexual attitudes, not from prudery but from a grounded fear of male sexual predation. There is in her writing of this period shock, disapproval, a lack of understanding of what younger women were up to. She seems to struggle mightily not to give way to bitterness and a sense of betrayal. The measure of her disappointment has to be taken against the historical background of the struggle for suffrage: It took seventy-two years of ceaseless agitation on the part of millions of men and women to win an elementary civil right for half the population in what Woodrow Wilson (who overtly supported but covertly opposed woman suffrage) insisted on calling "the world's greatest democracy."[3]

Another example: the profound ambivalence felt by the Old Left for the New Left during the antiwar activity of the late 1960s and early 1970s. Having survived blacklists, slander, vilification, and the Smith Act, not to mention another profound postwar shift to the right—nearly twenty years of reaction and stagnation—the sight of thousands of dissidents, even self-styled Marxists in the streets should have filled the hearts of the Old Left to overflowing. But nothing of the kind happened. Communication between these two radical generations was difficult indeed. We in the New Left condemned their blind adherence to policies made in the Kremlin, their defense of some of the worst excesses of communist rule in the Soviet Union and China, their clear political irrelevance; they, in turn, could not understand the New Left's emphasis on personal politics which they thought was bourgeois and self-indulgent. They believed (rightly as it turned out) that our support of the idea of sexual revolution and of a hippie counterculture would alienate ordinary working people. They were shocked by our heretical belief (there was of course considerable disagreement about this within the New Left itself) that all forms of oppression were not reducible to class oppression. I myself have sympathy for the predicament of these Old Leftists, if not their politics. They waited twenty years for the word to be given, then the word was indeed given but it was the wrong word.

My own politics are frozen in time as well: I live still with the utopian hopes of the late 1960s. While the women's movement is alive, if not altogether well, the mass-based interracial coalition that ended apartheid in this country is quite dead and has been for many years; the Civil Rights movement was a crucible in which many of us were formed; it was a generational experience, no longer properly understood by anyone under sixty, repudiated by an influential Black separatist movement and regarded by many younger people of both races as a failure. I hear on the Nightly Business Report how well our country is doing, but then I see in my mind's eye what the U.S. Department of Labor has identified as eight out of nine of the country's poorest neighborhoods. These eight neighborhoods are all public housing projects in Chicago, where thousands of poor people are warehoused in near genocidal conditions. How can this be invisible to the media, and to virtually everyone else? I can communicate to almost no one, certainly not to young students or even to those whom I think ought to be sharing it, my dream of a new awakening, a revitalized multiracial Civil Rights movement that now has *redistribution* on its agenda. I might be from Mars or drifting somewhere on an ice floe.

III. The Loss of Intellectual Relevance and of the Tradition of Elder Wisdom

I am beginning to see now how the losses I have discussed are joined. My political ideas are obsolescent: as ideas solely, one can debate them; but another debate is not what I want, which is a peaceful, but paralyzing in its numbers, rerun of civil disobedience, an uprising by and for the "wretched of the earth."

I cannot think of intellectual obsolescence, without remembering my first year in graduate school, at UCLA. I think too of the cruelty of the young toward the old. There were old professors in my graduate department who were frozen intellectually in what had been fashionable in the very early days of their careers; we made fun of them, not knowing that such a fate might well befall us. I took a course with one of these professors, largely to escape having to take what were then the typical offerings of the department: seminars in which the conventions of "ordinary language" would be closely interrogated in order to dissolve philosophical problems (all of which were seen to arise when we let our language go "on holiday"), or else seminars in which all manner of philosophical issues would be quantified and then treated as exercises in logic. But the cure was as bad as the disease: we read Santayana and nothing but Santayana for fifteen weeks. I am perhaps the only living American philosopher who has read all four volumes of *The Life of Reason*, a very dull book.

The same thing is happening to me. I have tried to re-tool in order to figure out (and then only very imperfectly) what poststructuralists are talking about. I feel how strong is the tendency to stay with what I know and what I know how to teach, rather than have to assimilate ideas in what feels to me like an often impenetrable philosophical jargon. To the extent that I am able to do this, I find repetitions of ideas that have been articulated earlier, or else preposterous claims presented without argument. While I have profited from my encounter with Derrida, Foucault, and Judith Butler, I still have extraordinary difficulty getting through this stuff, just as my old professor had trouble getting beyond Santayana. But continental philosophy (my official area) and feminist theory have clearly undergone paradigm shifts. I cannot help but view this with a very jaundiced eye, but this can easily make me intellectually obsolete insofar as graduate students are concerned; they seem to take to much of this more easily than I do. Two dilemmas arise from such a situation: (a) Do I try to stay trendy, "with it," abandoning issues I think are more important or do I isolate myself, like those few older professors at UCLA who seemed intellectually to have outlived themselves? The "mastery" of such obscure figures as Deleuze, Guattari, Kristeva, Levinas, Jean-Luc Nancy, etc., is not something that one can just pick up in one's spare time. The other dilemma is really a moral one: (b) Even if my university has no mandatory retirement age, at what point should I step aside so as to give some younger philosopher with younger ideas a chance? Given the current dismal state of the academic job market, this is a question that academics over sixty, indeed well-situated older people in other professions as well, ought to be asking themselves.

Intellectual obsolescence can come to people who are not professional intellectuals. My late mother-in-law, for example, could never get it through her head that meat and other substantial, high-cholesterol, and wildly fattening foods weren't good for you. She stuffed us full of high fat delicious stuff at family dinners, but worse, she insisted (really) that we take at least two shopping bags full of the same kinds of food home with us. She had mastered the art of passive-aggressive manipulation so thoroughly that we were no match for her. For years I fed a friend's family of four out of those shopping bags; then they moved away and we had somehow to eat all this ourselves (for it's a sin to waste food). We avoided going to Teresa's for dinner; this only made us feel guiltier and more inclined to overeat when we were there, for she always pressed us to overeat.

Teresa was born to a family of landowning peasants in Lithuania. To be large and strong for a woman was a good thing: strong women made better field hands. Meat made you strong. At the age of sixteen, during the Second World War, she was kidnapped out of a field and taken to Germany to work in a factory. I cannot imagine what her diet was like there; after the war, she found herself in a camp for displaced persons where she married a man with a similar history.

They were sent to England where her only child, my husband, was born. She soon divorced his brutal father, finding herself without much English, without an education, and with a child to raise, this during the postwar austerity in England. She got a job in a sweatshop and managed somehow to put food on the table for herself and her son. In the fullness of time, she emigrated to Chicago, got a decent paying job, and was able to buy and cook as much food as she liked. She read nothing but the Bible and religious tracts, knew English, but never read the paper or watched television. While she knew that the two of us had, between us, six college degrees, we could never get it through the head of this woman who had faced starvation, perhaps for long periods of time, that meat, especially the high-quality, well-marbled kind that she was at last able to afford, could kill you. She could not understand why we were trying to eat vegetarian, why we wanted to avoid butter, cheese, and cream; surely, these were just crazy American ideas; lots of things about life in America seemed quite crazy to her.

A word about the loss of the wisdom tradition. In many societies, indeed, in earlier incarnations of our own, older people were regarded as wiser than the young, as proper arbiters of behavior, as moral authorities. The prestige of this role undoubtedly compensated for some of the losses that beset older people. Since many of these sages, even in male-dominated societies, were women, some feminists are trying to rescue the tradition of older women's wisdom, the wisdom of the "crone." But in our society, older people are not repositories of wisdom; they are seen more often as superannuated, out of step with the times, hopelessly old-fashioned. This is, unfortunately, often the case, as whatever wisdom the elderly have gathered belongs to a different historical moment. Ours is not a traditional culture in which values are preserved from one generation to another. (This is tied, I think to the rapid alteration and manipulation of needs and values that is required by a voracious consumer capitalism.) My mother and her friends, for example, were genuinely shocked and mildly outraged that feminine hygiene products were advertised openly on television. Both my parents thought that premarital sex was morally wrong, though sex was so little discussed in our house that I never found out exactly what *was* wrong with it. They were of course completely disapproving of "living in sin" (even though both were atheists and didn't believe in sin) and even though they had close friends, who, because they were of different religions and didn't have the courage to stand down their families, lived "in sin" for years. My parents even tried to discourage me from going to a man's apartment alone. This puzzled me until, much later, I began to see many 1930s films on the *Late Show* in which the same morality was at work: going alone to a man's apartment raised the very real suspicion that you would spend the night with him. I suppose that they were worried that I would lose what they believed to be a major asset on the marriage market: my virginity.

IV. The Loss of the Significant Other

As women live longer than men, the coupled heterosexual woman can, statistically, look forward to widowhood. The loss and the loneliness are no less, of course, for lesbians. I have seen several women set free by widowhood: women whose caretaking of sick, dependent, childish, or querulous old men was burdensome in the extreme. At the end of life, they find themselves doing something akin to childcare. My neighbor, Noann, became a prisoner in her own home: whenever she tried to go shopping or to the hairdresser, her husband (whose mind was gone) would begin to wail so loudly and so piteously at the sight of the "sitter" that Noann's heart would soften and she would stay home, sending the sitter to buy the groceries. Noann's sense of duty and her feminine socialization into self-sacrifice was such that she wouldn't consider sending her husband to a nursing home; hence, in spite of the fact that this couple was quite well off, Noann allowed herself to be put under house arrest for nearly five years and she was only set free by his death.

And then there were Sarah and Jake. Jake was a cigar chomping, enormous man physically; his bulk seemed to fill all available space. He was kindly, funny, with a loud, booming voice that filled any space that may still have remained. He was an accomplished raconteur who grabbed the center of attention wherever he found himself. Sara was a smaller woman, somewhat lumpish, with rounded shoulders and a body language that spoke of defeat. She had plucked her eyebrows almost all out, 1930s style and had penciled in two deeply curving lines above her eyes that spoke eloquently of sadness. Sarah always walked behind Jake, because he was too large to go through a doorway *with* anyone else. He seemed always to ignore her, which encouraged everyone else to ignore her too. Since she couldn't speak when Jake was there (nor could anyone else), it was assumed that she had nothing to say.

In the fullness of time. Jake died. When Jake died, Sarah came alive. She was found to have a voice, opinions, wit, and funny stories of her own. Was Jake, this kindly and generous man, really a succubus who had been feeding on her substance for fifty years? She began standing straighter. She totally revised her eyebrows. She bought a new wardrobe of light print dresses, just right for Miami Beach to which she removed herself at the earliest opportunity—a suggestion Jake had always vetoed. She went to tea dances for "Senior Citizens" and hinted, on her trips back to Chicago, of a life devoted, if not to dalliance, then to flirting.

But these are not representative tales. For most of the widowed, male and female, there is, in all likelihood, profound grief and loneliness. Two things we need to flourish are taken away: the affirming gaze of the Other and the comfort of physical touching. It has been well documented that infants deprived of touching and physical contact can fail to flourish. Something of this sort is true of adults too, though its deprivation does not have the dire consequences it has for infants. I was once separated from my Significant Other for six months. I realized after several months that I was suffering from something that I had never seen described: it was a *skin hunger*. It wasn't sex that I missed so much as the comfort of a warm body in bed, the feeling of being held and stroked—touched. I had at that time a sudden insight into one of the many deprivations attendant on institutionalization—the deprivation of a loving touch. Fortunate are the elderly who have grandchildren who will sit on their laps and let themselves be petted and cossetted. Some isolated older people are advised to buy dogs and the advice seems to be quite sound, yet sad. How can a terrier stand in for your beloved? The idea that my life's companion will die before I do fills me with the same dread I have at the prospect of my own death. Yet, I believe that he will suffer terribly if I die first and he is left alone. This sums up so much about aging: a lose-lose situation.

V. The Loss of the Gaze

One of our needs is of course to see, but also to be seen and to be seen as attractive or, at least, as not repulsive. If Significant Others know how to please their lovers, they will remark, from time to time, on how attractive is their self-presentation. At seventy-two, my mother could expect appreciative comments from my father on her appearance; perhaps this was one of the secrets of their long and happy life together. Unless there is someone who sees you, and will tell you that you or at least some part of your costume, is attractive or stylish, you run the risk of invisibility. Feeling invisible, being made invisible, is, for anyone who has passed through middle age, a familiar experience, superbly described in Doris Lessing's *Summer Before the Dark*.[4] At a certain point I noticed that strangers had lost interest in talking to me. When I was younger and more attractive, I had all kinds of lively conversations in the grocery line, the line at the movies, etc. Some of these conversations were initiated by me, most by men. Now, no one begins a conversation with me and, when I myself start the conversation I get a polite reply and then silence; the conversation is ended and with it, metaphorically speaking, so is my existence for the other. What surprised me about this is not that men lost interest in speaking to me, but that young women did too. Young women are interested in each other, but not, so it appears, in women in middle age.

I have written elsewhere and at some length about women's embodiment in advanced industrial society (see, in this volume, "Suffering to Be Beautiful" [chapter 1]). The anxieties we have as young women often grow worse in middle age, but what about old age? This is something about which we know very little. I suspect that old age is welcomed by some women because the *issue* of one's appearance has been settled; one is now an unattractive old crow and that's the end of it. Invisibility is incompatible with any but the most cursory appraisal, hence we no longer need to impose on ourselves the disciplinary regime of idealized embodied femininity. But I suspect that many older women have the same needs and anxieties they had in middle age and as young commodities on the "Meet Market" and we know that many older women are still consumers of the accoutrements of the fashion-beauty complex.[5] The gaze of the beloved other is now no more: what then? Giving the whole thing up is certainly a reasonable response but so too is the demand that we be seen with some appreciation. Many women have invented a strategy to secure their appearance in spite of the disappearance of the gaze of the singular beloved Other as well as (at best) the indifference of the generalized social other, but before I proceed to describe this strategy, some consideration should be given to a related issue much neglected (at least in feminist theory): the sexuality of older women.

Masters and Johnson did everyone, not just the elderly, a great service in finding that neither sexual capacity (especially in women, but in men too) nor sexual enjoyment must necessarily cease with aging.[6] But a number of obstacles stand in the way of the elderly's full utilization of this finding. First, there is, for the heterosexual woman, the fact that the ratio of women to men in every passing decade increases, this due to the fact that men die younger than women. Second, there is the folk belief that sexual interest disappears with age, indeed, that it *should* disappear and that the continuation in the aged of a keen sexual interest, not to mention an active sex life, is not just inappropriate, but faintly disreputable. I suppose that this idea had its origin in the belief that sex was for reproduction only, but hardly anyone in this country still believes this. Geriatric sex seems always good for a laugh in the entertainment media. Not long ago I spoke with a friend in California whose mother, aged ninety-three, lives (assisted) in a posh senior citizen complex. Her mother likes it there very much, but she complains about the dearth of available men. My friend laughed at this and so did I. It seemed then (only last week) that laughter was appropriate, but now that I have set myself the task of reflecting upon aging, I'm not so sure. Now I feel guilty for having colluded in this act of condescension. Finally, I believe that some elderly persons, particularly women, remove themselves from the admittedly slim chance of dalliance because of the belief that sex and romance are the reward of youth and beauty. The old and ugly do not deserve, or cannot hope to generate sexual desire in another. While there is always talk about the beauty of older women's deeply lined faces (mostly from artists and photographers) most people know better. Sexiness and youth are conjoined continually in films, advertising, music videos, magazines. I suspect that there is also the belief that any halfway desirable man could get a younger woman if he tried and that younger women are more adventurous in bed, more up-to-date in their sexual technique. There is no evidence that this is the case: what we have here is a socially depreciated self colluding in its own depreciation, a classic self-fulfilling prophecy: the patriarchal gaze turned inward.

On being seen: some women have invented strategies to see and be seen. I live next door to a large apartment building, a large percentage of whose residents are elderly widows. While I think that many are quite lonely, it is also the case that they have made some sort of society for themselves, going together on a direct downtown express bus to concerts, shopping, and the theater. I take this bus often myself. What these women have done, quite subversively, and, I am sure unconsciously, is to create an approving and appreciative collective gaze with which they affirm one another. They really look at one another, noticing what is new, or what is changed. "I love what you've done with your hair," they say to one another; "What a gorgeous suit, is it new?" "You're looking wonderful, Sophie, have you lost weight?" They are delighted and excited to see one another; they have created a new gaze, not the gaze of standard-issue patriarchy or of dead husbands, but a democratic and inclusive gaze that installs something attractive in everyone. This is a tribute to the unplanned ingenuity of aging women to restore to themselves what the culture has taken away—their self-esteem, their dignity, their beauty.

VI. Fear of the Loss of Physical and Mental Capacity; Fear of Death

I have saved the worst for last. The loss of one's mental capacities is perhaps more of a nightmare than the loss or impairment of physical function. Senile dementia from any cause, Alzheimer's disease—these strike fear into our hearts because, like death, they are a loss of self and a permanent loss of the world. Horror show: I turn into a baby, then into a vegetable. Another horror show: I have a series of strokes that leave me almost totally paralyzed and unable to speak, but my mind is clear. Horrible too is the idea that such things could happen on a schedule that wouldn't allow me sufficient capacity to arrange my own suicide. Could my father's relentless cheerfulness find a silver lining here? I do not believe that these are situations that can be redeemed unless, perhaps, one has perfect religious faith. Faith, in the Christian theological tradition, is a gift of God and it is not a gift that He or She has given to me. For those of us without faith, we can try only not to dwell upon calamities that might not occur after all and try to make some provision to protect those close to us in case they do.

Other dramatic losses, e.g., blindness and deafness, are terrible too. At what age should we begin to re-read the Stoics? My father's deafness made it impossible for him to hear anything that was said if there was background noise, e.g., at a party. Music, which he loved very much, sounded increasingly distorted. I myself have macular degeneration of the optic nerve, so it is a question whether I shall go blind before I die or die before I go blind. One wishes for a serene death, but there are terrible ways of dying; we hope to find courage to get through it. But get through it we must, with or without courage.

Living as I do, surrounded by the elderly, I see daily less dramatic signs of decay: wizened old ladies creeping along inside their walkers; grim-faced old women, mouths tightened against pain, being wheeled about by their caretakers. These elderly women do not smile; they are intent on surviving the outing; they sometimes snap at their caretakers who are made to bear the brunt of their client's bitterness and frustration. Sometimes, but not often, one sees what looks like friendship between a white-uniformed nurse and her charge. The caretakers are not registered nurses though a few are LPNs. Most of the caretakers now are black, undocumented Polish women or Filippinas. One wonders how they deal with the monotony of their work, the poor pay, and, as they must live anywhere from twelve to twenty-four hours a day with their charges, the loneliness and isolation. The elderly women are fortunate in having the means to keep their own small apartments and to hire the assistance they need; their grown daughters are off the hook and because of the sexual division of labor, the sons typically escape daily caretaking responsibility too. They are able to live surrounded by objects that are invested with memory and saturated with meaning. The transition to a nursing home strips a woman of most of her possessions, hence of important links to her past and her place in the order of things that had made up her world. The fateful but apparently innocent, indeed necessary, requirement of institutionalization is part of the extinction of identity that leads sooner or later to death.

I have been considering some of the probable losses of old age, only one of which is absolutely certain, death; death is not a loss like other losses: it is not a process we live through or live with. It is almost certain that most of us have already or will suffer some measure of disability, though many elderly people die with their capacities intact. Further, as Anita Silvers and Susan

Wendell have so eloquently shown, "disability" is to an extent relative to the capacity of the built environment to enable persons with physical limitations to participate in the ordinary business of life.[7] I have pondered the isolation and loneliness of the aged: this too is relative to a person's situation. Her friends may have lived on into old age, her children might be unusually attentive, her husband might confound the statistics and outlive her. The losses to which I directed most of my attention—the loss of one's social and professional networks, loss of a hopeful vision of the future, intellectual obsolescence, loss of the social convention that ascribed wisdom, hence moral authority to the aged, loss of conventional physical attractiveness, and finally, the loss of opportunities for romantic and sexual experience—these losses are social, not biological. But this does not mean that they are easily overcome. My aim in trying to identify some major losses involved in the process of aging is to start a conversation about what we can anticipate as we age and what steps we can take to eliminate these losses or at least to soften their effect.

How to deal with the loss of social and professional networks? It is necessary for professional networks to be open to younger people; this means that criteria for inclusion must be flexible. In order to do "outreach" one must be prepared to see the network altered and enlarged. This means that the older age cohort will have to learn to share control. Also, the network must show younger persons that it can and will help them professionally. The Radical Philosophy Association is a good example of a supportive and sustaining network of friends and colleagues of different ages and career stages. One's small professional circle may be devastated by death; what this means is that we must anticipate that this will happen and help to create ongoing organizations that will still be in place for us as we age. The best guarantee that we will feel at home in these groups is if we give them our support now. Where networks do not exist, elderly people who feel alienated and "out of it" need to organize, for surely, there are other old people who are feeling the same way. And the critical mass necessary for the success of a network—or just a "support group"—can be quite small. I have never understood why people often say proudly, "I'm not a joiner." Ice floe ahead.

The Wednesday girls were, I believe, victims of institutional heterosexuality. Even though their network was, for many, far more sustaining than their marriages, they were compelled to define marriage and family as primary. Hence, instead of moving even closer to one another as they aged and/or were widowed, they made the conventional moves with and for their husbands, or toward their adult children. Given who they were and when they lived, this was inevitable. But their fate is, at least for me, exemplary: they held friendship too cheaply. For me their stories are tied to questions about how we want to retire and with whom and what sorts of arrangements we need to be making now. Do we want to face the necessity of fitting ourselves into some retirement community with people who do not share our interests or values? Do we want to leave behind networks of friends and family to go off with just a partner to points south? What kinds of stress would this put on the relationship? How well would we flourish, sundered from so many of the people who have sustained us? Or do we want to begin to think now about shaping our own retirement communities, or settlements, or communes? We need to do something extraordinary: we need to imagine alternative institutional arrangements, new ways of living together that might never have been tried before. This task is particularly urgent for people like me who have no children, as well as people who have families but won't want to live with them in later life. Charlotte Perkins Gilman re-imagined domesticity in extremely unusual ways; we need to do the same for "retirement communities."

Intellectual obsolescence: a tough call. Assume that old dogs *can* be taught new tricks. Find a class or pay a tutor to come to your home and teach you effective computer-literacy. Skim a respectable journal of opinion so that you can become conversant (more or less) with controversies, fads, and fashions in the worlds of science, the arts, and letters. When I was younger I was obsessed with the need to be always *au courant*, now I don't care. I have a colleague who chides me because I think it valuable to do cultural critique, yet don't stay current with fashionable rap or rock groups and television sitcoms. It is unclear to me how conversant we need to be with the pop culture of youth.

My own field, philosophy, is tossed about on the seas of fashion too. Who would have predicted, for example, during the heyday of positivism that there would be a revival of Hegel among analytical philosophers? Or that we would have to rebut the extreme nominalism that one encounters among some poststructuralists? That there are those who call themselves feminists yet doubt that there are "women"? We should refuse to have to be always *au courant*; we have devoted decades to our own intellectual development, to determining where we are, what we believe, and what we think is important in the field. We should be true to ourselves, not tossed hither and yon by every new intellectual fashion. Now this can be a problem, especially if we are teachers. I sweated blood one whole summer over Derrida principally so that I could teach him. This was not wasted effort as some of what Derrida has to say is interestingly disturbing (though ultimately, I think, wrong). Here too we need tutors: give the text a chance and if it does not reveal its meaning, and you cannot afford or find a human tutor, get a stack of secondary sources and keep looking until you find one that makes some sense of what you read; you have found a teacher. One of the professional networks to which I belong does internal education from time to time: someone with the appropriate interest will volunteer to explain the teaching of some newer, trendy figure. Since this person from our network will be a friend who will volunteer to answer questions we might pose much later, we have found a network that has within it a teacher. Now all of this just complicates the juggling act that is our professional life: it is difficult to know if an extremely demanding job just increases the stress as one ages and is part of what will ultimately kill us, or if the challenge uses and even augments our powers, thereby keeping us alive longer.

On the disappearance of the elder wisdom tradition: I do not know if younger people find me wise or not. Some younger students, I'm sure, find my ideas quaint and quite superannuated. I share with my graduate students the ordeals I faced as a graduate student and a junior faculty member, hoping that they can learn something from my experience. Mostly they listen politely but noncommittally. I notice that when they are in crisis or need advice they tend to go to younger faculty.

Now others may not believe that we are wise, but some of us know that we are wiser than we were when we were younger. Some older people are just as foolish as they were when they were younger. I too am capable of major stupidities but I believe too that I am more mature, more serene, more accepting of my own limitations, less obsessed with issues of success and failure and with what other people will think of me than I used to be, in a word, less self-absorbed. In the fullness of time, the story gets told. We are not beset with crises of identity: we know now what we decided to do with our lives; we know (though even self-knowledge is not always reliable) what we have turned into or turned ourselves into. We know whether we decided, in the end, to have children or not, and if we did, we know how they turned out. Most of our careers are already behind us: we know what we did and what we didn't do and there's no point in agonizing over our competence or lack of it now. Indecision and lack of confidence are twin tormentors of youth, but not as often of age.

On the question of disappointment with politics, or the course of history: this is a particular issue for those of us who lived excitedly through a period of change and experimentation but who find ourselves stranded in a profoundly conservative epoch. This disillusionment is perhaps the kind of thing that lies at the root of the bitterness one encounters sometimes in old people, this or the sense that life has cheated them, or both. But unless one has accepted some form of historical determinism, we need to regard the future as open. After all, who among us believed that the system that seemed so totally in control of the Soviet Union would collapse so quickly, so totally, and so completely that, in the end, not even its leadership would defend it? Imagine too how impregnable the system of Jim Crow must have looked to both blacks and whites in the South the day before Rosa Parks refused to give up her seat on the bus to a white man. We may have, as Gramsci put it, "pessimism of the intellect," but we need also "optimism of the will." I have not heard much lately about the Gray Panthers. If they are in decline, we should be prepared to reinvigorate them: nothing banishes political despair so well as a good fight. And I am enormously impressed with the good work done by OWL, the Older Women's League. This will be there for us later if we support it now. I spoke earlier about the need, even for the elderly for teachers and tutors: we will need role-models as well. Bertrand Russell, Jean-Paul Sartre, Simone de Beauvoir, and many others cared passionately about the fate of the world that they were about to leave. Their lives bear study.

I come finally to the appearance of the elderly and to their sexuality. The usual fund of experience out of which people write about such things, "things that are for the most part so" (Aristotle) is not available to me. There are no fashion magazines aimed at women in their seventies, or special sections devoted to their dress in department stores. My own mother died at seventy-two. She and her friends were very concerned with appearance, but no more, that I could detect, than they were in their forties or fifties. There are no reports of widespread anorexia or bulimia in elderly women. A friend's mother described to me her sense of alienation when she would glimpse herself in a mirror. She felt young inside, she said, but her face was criss-crossed with deep lines of age. I myself have the same experience, but with fewer lines; I am shocked by the aging of my body, not just my face. Older women are not expected to "make the most of what they have": they have escaped the requirements of ideal embodied femininity and are now supposed to become invisible, to dwindle away into retirement villages or nursing homes or to respond selflessly to the demands of the day-care crisis by caretaking their grandchildren or even great-grandchildren.

I have written elsewhere about the need for a revolutionary aesthetics of the body; insofar as this has not yet appeared, we must live in the world as it is. I saluted earlier the ingenuity of the older women of the Sheridan Road bus who subverted the social depreciation of aging women's bodies by becoming, each one, an enthusiastic witness for the others' bodily being.

I shall close with a fantasy I have about these women, my neighbors in a huge and faceless 1950s high-rise like so many other such buildings, with similar populations, that line Chicago's northerly lakefront. My fantasy would offend many deeply, some perhaps not at all. While these women have made a sort of society for one another, each lives alone; I believe that many are lonely in the way one is lonely who has friends, but lacks a certain kind of intimacy. I believe too that many have what I called earlier "skin hunger." Here is my fantasy: these elderly widows abandon their deeply entrenched homophobia (for they too, like the Wednesday girls, are victims of institutionalized heterosexuality) and, just as they have learned to meet each other's needs for visibility and affirmation, they go one step further and begin to meet each other's needs for physical intimacy. This intimacy need not be sexual, but if it is sexual, so much the better. Perhaps there are women whose needs extend no farther than hugging and embracing, frequent nuzzling kisses, the comfort of a warm body touching one's own body in bed on a winter night. For the women who need sex and have not had it for decades, I fantasize wild sexual excitement and fulfillment and the special kind of confidence that comes with the knowledge that one has the capacity to arouse sexual desire in another. Their condo would come alive with couplings and the rumors of couplings, dalliance, flirting, gossip, matchmaking, lovers' quarrels, and *liaisons innocentes ou dangereuses*. Now these suddenly energetic sisters will have more to talk about than the day's ration of soap operas or the terminal cuteness of their grandchildren. An army of elderly Amazons: watch out!

Notes

This chapter was previously published in *Mother Time: Women, Aging, and Ethics*, edited by Margaret Urban Walker (Lanham, Md.: Rowman & Littlefield, 1999).

1. The idea that the stages of life are "socially constructed" came to me principally from two sources: Philippe Aries, *Centuries of Childhood: A Social History of Family Life*, trans. Robert Baldrick (New York: Alfred A. Knopf, 1962); and Margaret Morganroth Gullett's recent path-breaking "deconstruction" of middle age, *Declining to Decline, Cultural Combat and the Politics of the Midlife* (Charlottesville and London: University Press of Virginia, 1997).

2. The 1980 *Diagnostic and Statistical Manual of Mental Disorders III* no longer lists homosexuality as a form of mental illness.

3. It was only the white female half of the population that actually got the vote: black men and women were disenfranchised throughout the South. The women's movement colluded in the racism of the period: believing that it could not afford to alienate white Southern voters and politicians, the National American Women's Suffrage Association raised no objection to Jim Crow; moreover in deference to the "sensibilities" of the white ladies of the South, it refused to seat black delegates to its conventions.

4. Doris Lessing, *Summer Before the Dark* (New York: Alfred A. Knopf, 1973).

5. See Bartky, "Narcissism, Femininity and Alienation," in *Femininity and Domination: Studies in the Phenomenology of Oppression* (New York: Routledge, 1990).

6. William H. Masters and Virginia E. Johnson, *Human Sexual Response* (Boston: Little Brown and Co., 1966).

7. Susan Wendell, *The Rejected Body: A Feminist Philosophical Reflection on Disease* (New York: Routledge, 1996); Anita Silvers, "Aging Fairly: Feminist and Disability Perspectives in Intergenerational Justice," in *Mother Time: Women, Aging, and Ethics*, ed. Margaret Urban Walker (Lanham, Md.: Rowman & Littlefield, 1999), 203–226.

~

CHAPTER SIX

Phenomenology of a Hyphenated Consciousness

I. Growing Up Jewish in America

Are there patterns in the construction of personal identities? What part is played by dominant discourses that tell me who I ought to be and my acceptance, rejection, or most often, my personal re-configuration of such discourses? This question is particularly acute when we ask it about minority or marginalized groups, since the center, that regards itself as the rational, the normal, and, with some exceptions, the admirable, identifies itself in opposition to the margins, wherein dwell the nonrational, the abnormal, the unusual, and, very often, the undesirable. I think that there are patterns in the construction, both personal and social, of both mainstream and minority identities, though it would take a major research project to ferret them all out. In the autobiographical narrative that follows, I shall describe one such pattern, my own, which I call "dialectical." I shall briefly characterize other patterns and in the final section of the chapter I shall consider some ethical issues that present themselves in the course of considering how viable personal identities can be salvaged from an initial position of abjection.

Postmodernists are right, I think, to regard identities as "multiple," even as "fragmented." They do not mean by this (although sometimes it sounds as if they do) that we suffer from multiple personality disorder but that everyone bears a large number of social inscriptions and that some part of our behavior may well be unconsciously motivated, hence all but impervious to rational control. Thus, I am a woman, a teacher, also in certain situations, a student, a lover, a daughter, a sister, a registered Democrat, a lover of antiques, a member of the Society for the Preservation of Old Theater Organs, etc. Some aspects of my identity I choose; some I do not. There is no way that I can choose not to have been born a Jew in what is often referred to as a "Christian country." I can try to pass, as was done more commonly in my parents' generation, but in such a case, I am still a Jew, now a "Jew-passing." What follows is the story of my own appropriation of a Jewish-American identity.

East European Jews were among the most stigmatized people of Christian Europe; their stigmatized status did not disappear when they disembarked at Ellis Island. I grew up Jewish in the 1940s and 1950s in a prosperous, safe, attractive, and heavily (but not entirely) Jewish community on the northwest side of Chicago. While my parents had a large circle of both Jewish and Gentile friends, and even though there had been considerable intermarriage on both sides of my family, Gentiles were still a curiosity to me. Two of my Gentile aunts, Rita and Peggy, were particular curiosities, especially Peggy, stunning in her little black hat with its half-veil, her doll-like beauty, her red-red lipstick, her mink and diamonds, trailing behind her a heady aroma of expensive perfume and cigarette smoke. Both Peggy and Rita drank Scotch in the afternoon. The Jewish matrons in the neighborhood found smoking (for a woman) a bit "fast" and drank nothing but a little sacramental wine at Passover. My uncles, the husbands of these aunts, had been successful bootleggers, hence, had their choice of the choicest women of the demimonde.

There were anti-Semites in the neighborhood as well. The man across the street got drunk regularly, threw up his window, and shouted anti-Semitic slurs with such force that they could be heard up and down the block. There was a Catholic school nearby and some of the boys, on their way home, would sometimes taunt my brother and me with anti-Semitic slogans ("dirty Jews"), and throw stones or snowballs at us. But as the neighborhood became increasingly Jewish, the enrollment at St. Timothy's shrank, our tormentors disappeared, and the drunken anti-Semite across the way moved as well. Perhaps he moved to Sauganash, a community west of us of more beautiful homes than ours (our neighborhood consisted mostly of two- and three-flat apartments). Sauganash was "restricted," which meant that deeds to the properties there specified that they could only be transferred to Christians. Shortly after the end of the Second World War, the Supreme Court declared real estate "restrictive covenants" unconstitutional.

Toward the end of the war, photographs of the death camps began appearing in the papers. All that was exposed had been rumored, but not in such ghastly detail. My father had been skeptical. As a boy during World War I, he and many other Americans, had been taken in by trumped-up atrocity stories

("Huns cutting off the hands of Belgian children") and he wasn't about to be taken in again. But the photographs and eye-witness accounts left no doubt about the horror of the Holocaust. The reaction in my household to pictures of the crematoria and to bodies stacked like cordwood was one of shock and horror. My parents' horrified response was as much a response to the recognition that such barbarities as these could be inflicted on anyone as to the fact that a disproportionate number of the victims were Jews.

My parents, like most of our neighbors, were children of immigrants, climbing rapidly into the middle and upper-middle class. Their lives were a balancing act between assimilation into mainstream American society and loyalty to Jewish tradition. My parents were atheists. They were also very strongly Jewish-identified. Their identification was not with a religion but with an ethnicity and a history. The state of Israel was founded when I was thirteen; this—and the balancing act of most American Jews—gave momentum to a question that had agitated much of Jewry for decades: What is a Jew? Did all Jews have an obligation to emigrate to Israel and help build a national homeland? Could one be a Jew but not a Zionist? Could one be a Jew and an atheist?

My father's answers to these questions became my own. My father, a very brilliant man, was the major intellectual influence on the first twenty years of my life. He was very much a Jew of the Diaspora, whose intellectual roots were in the Enlightenment and, like many Jewish intellectuals of his generation, in German culture of the nineteenth and early twentieth century. He had respect for the tradition of Jewish learning but little real interest in it. He gave generously to Jewish relief organizations but also to worthy non-Jewish causes. He supported the founding of the state of Israel as a homeland for other Jews, not for us. We were Jews, but also Americans.

My only Jewish education was given me at home, at the Passover service and ritual meal, the Seder. My father made what I consider an exemplary Seder, neither too long nor too short. He recited many prayers in Hebrew, so that we could hear the sound of the ancestral tongue, but the bulk of the service was in English. We circled the table, everyone reading passages from the Haggadah, the ritual service. He hit the high spots and avoided the rabbinical commentary: nothing crucial was omitted from the embellished story of the Exodus: the ten plagues, the four questions, the wise, simple, and wicked sons, the "*dyanus*."[1] All the ritual foods were displayed and some were eaten—of course the matzoh, the unleavened bread, the bitter herb, symbolizing the bitterness of exile and slavery, the charoseth, a finely chopped mixture of nuts, apples, and wine, that symbolized the mortar with which the Jews were said to have built the pyramids. The service is punctuated by the drinking of sweet sacramental wine: the first time, never to be forgotten, that a Jewish child is allowed to partake of alcohol. The Haggadah instructs us to imagine that it was not those distant peoples, but *ourselves* who were delivered out of slavery in Egypt; indeed, the point of the service is not only to praise God for deliverance, but to remember the event in its entirety, indeed to try to relive it: "It is incumbent upon every Israelite in every generation to imagine if he had actually gone out from Egypt."[2] In the tradition of the rabbis, my father would discourse briefly on the meaning of the text. This varied from year to year, but mostly, he saw in it, as I see in it too, a joyful and universal message about freedom and the emancipation from slavery.[3]

Attention would then shift from father to mother, who served an enormous traditional meal (most of the time she cooked American)—from matzoh ball soup and gefilte fish to the towering Passover sponge cake, a triumph made entirely without yeast. After her mother died, my mother, with joyous relief, stopped keeping a kosher kitchen. Keeping kosher is a difficult and complex business. Although she had what I would call a more "tribal" sense than my father, she damned traditional orthodox practices, even Jewish religious beliefs, as "superstitious" or "medieval."

In spite of his strong Jewish identity, my father had an ecumenical turn of mind. He had studied the New Testament and found the moral teaching there somewhat more elevated than that of the Old Testament. And, we celebrated Christmas: I think that I have never had a Jewish friend who understood or approved of this but without it, my childhood would have been deprived of some of its greatest joys. We celebrated Hanukkah as well. One, my father was fond of saying, is the celebration of victory in war, the other "the celebration of the birth of the Prince of Peace." The orthodox grandmothers had begun this, thinking that Santa Claus was an American figure and Christmas an American holiday. So my mother and father and their brothers and sisters hung up their stockings near the coal stove on Christmas eve.

Christmas alone was celebrated at school. We were taught mostly by female Irish-Catholic "losers" (old maids or widows) with two-year teaching degrees.[4] They never mentioned religion *per se*, but the school was decorated with wreaths and pine branches and portraits of Santa. We were taught all the Christmas carols. Imagine: forty-five children, forty-three of them Jewish, singing lustily of "Round John Virgin." Our parents, having still no sense of entitlement to a critique of American institutions, never complained.

My brother and I wrote letters to Santa, were taken to see the real Santa, i.e., the Santa at Marshall Field's, a huge figure bathed in dazzling light (for the snapshots) before whom we were struck dumb with awe. My father loved

Dickens' *A Christmas Carol* which he understood to contain the real values of Christmas—generosity, compassion, and good fellowship. He talked a good deal about the pagan origins of Christmas. On Christmas morning, my brother and I ran into the magically transformed living room. The presents, in two lines in front of the fireplace, his and mine, were arranged in order of ascending psychological impact with the most spectacular and unexpected at the end. Our stockings, hung up empty the night before, were full of candy canes and little toys and perhaps there would be a half-eaten sandwich and a thank-you note from Santa. But my father wouldn't have a Christmas tree: Christmas trees were for Gentiles. That is where *he* drew the line.

II. Denial and Apostasy

At sixteen, I went away to school, a large public university downstate. There I broke out of the largely homogeneous community in which I was raised and met a great diversity of students—from farms, small towns, foreign countries, and even the black South Side of Chicago. It was there and then that I came to feel my Jewish identity as burdensome.

There were many complex issues that I dealt with in the painful, prolonged (and, I suspect, typical) identity crisis of late adolescence and early adulthood. My Jewish identity was only one such issue and it was triggered by a long and agonized exchange of letters between myself and my parents having to do with the dating of Gentiles. My parents wanted me to promise that I wouldn't date Gentile boys. I resisted this. In spite of my father's cultural and intellectual ecumenism and in spite of their wide and mixed circle of friends, both my parents believed that deep down, unknown perhaps even to themselves, all Gentiles were anti-Semitic. Dating led eventually to marriage and one of their greatest fears was that I would marry outside of the group. Eventually I promised, tearfully, to do as they asked. Perhaps I meant it when I promised it, but in point of fact, I dated whom I pleased. In the course of my college career, it is true, I became seriously involved with two Jews, one a musician, the other a published poet. Each expected me to marry him, but I knew I'd marry neither. These men were so much like myself in background and in shared values, aesthetic, and intellectual preferences, even neuroses, that sex with either would have felt incestuous. This being the 1950s, one could be virtually engaged, and not have to "go the limit." I was secretly (and profoundly) attracted sexually to big blond jocks, utterly unlike my cerebral father and those Doppelgänger Jewish intellectuals. The two men with whom I (serially) have spent most of my adult life are not Jewish. An attraction to big, blond jocks: is this internalized anti-Semitism?[5]

I believe then that what I disliked most about being Jewish was the fact that I hadn't chosen it. I had been chosen by it. Furthermore, I would always be somewhat alien in my own country. This label—"Jewish-American"—would follow me all the rest of my life. I would never be a real American, always a hybrid; I wanted to live in my country as someone truly *of* the country, not as a perpetual hyphen, straddling margin and center. Mostly, I wanted to be free, free of all designations, free of all ascriptions, so that I could freely mold myself. Having not yet read Sartre, I did not know that the freedom I sought was impossible.

I discovered the Unitarian Church. A good number of faculty belonged and the congregation took stands on political issues that challenged the McCarthyism of the day. I myself was apolitical then, but I approved of the stands they took. The church which didn't look like a church was built in the "mission" or "bungalow" style that was popular earlier in this century. There were no religious images anywhere. God and Christ were present only in some of the traditional hymns we sang. The minister was an appealing young man who never mentioned God in his sermons; indeed, one Sunday's sermon consisted solely of a reading of Shelley's "Ode to the West Wind," that poem of hope that ends "If winter comes, can spring be far behind?" And Unitarianism was so *American*! It was founded in America by high-minded New Englanders—representatives of the American spirit at its best, as I then thought—as an alternative to the narrowness and intolerance of Puritanism.

I especially liked to dress up on Sunday morning and wobble down to church in my high-heels; this was what real Americans did, they went to church on Sunday morning. One Sunday morning there was a ceremony of joining that involved inscribing one's name in a huge book on a stand in front of the altar. I signed, thus officially joining the church.

Several months later, I spent a weekend with a friend in Hyde Park, in the neighborhood of the University of Chicago. There is a large Unitarian congregation in Hyde Park and so, on Sunday, I resolved to go to "my" church. This building looked just like a cathedral, indeed, it looked like the Episcopal church in Urbana, only bigger; and it looked nothing like the mission-style building where I had been hanging out. It was a huge gray stone affair, with high vaulted Gothic arches. The wooden church benches were carved with Gothic arches as well. There was an organ. The minister appeared, dressed in a floor-length black robe and a white collar. He ascended a spiral staircase to a pulpit, carved with the inevitable Gothic arches, from which he proceeded to conduct the service. A paralyzing thought slowly took shape in my mind: "Oh my God, I've joined a Protestant church!" I ran out of there, never to return, nor did I ever return to any Unitarian church, except for concerts. I have absolutely nothing against Unitarians and so I never thought to erase my name from the big book. And so ends a tale of "being in denial" that I would match against any told in Alcoholics Anonymous.

After graduation I was awarded a Fulbright Scholarship to Germany to study philosophy. I had no particular desire to go to Germany as opposed to, say, France or England, but one had to show competence in the language of the country to which one applies and the Fulbright Commission pretended that two years of college credit in a foreign language was evidence of competence, which of course, it is not. There was a contingency at work here. Thinking that every educated person should know, minimally, French and German, I went to register for French. But the lines at the French desk were extremely long and there was no one waiting at the German desk; so I registered for German. I was at the time in the College of Music, so German seemed an appropriate choice. Later, when I transferred to Liberal Arts, I had so many Liberal Arts graduation requirements to make up that I couldn't fit French into my schedule. Hence the extraordinary year in Germany, in which I passed as "Evangelisch," i.e., Protestant. Given my flirtation with Unitarianism, this was not entirely a lie. Why did I do it? Was I still in flight from a Jewish identity? Or was the reason I gave myself the real reason? I thought that if I signaled my Jewishness from the start, I would never know what Germans really thought about Jews, the War, and the Holocaust. What I discovered there I think I would have discovered after a year of passing in the United States: some Germans were guilt-ridden and conscience-stricken about what their parents had consented to (my German friends were mostly my age) while other Germans, apparently having learned nothing from the War, were anti-Semitic in fairly banal ways.[6]

I spent a semester in Munich and even though Dachau was now a war memorial, and only a short train ride away, I never went there. I was unwilling to open myself completely to what Jewish identity had meant to *those* Jews. I avoided reading Holocaust literature throughout most of my adult life.

III. Two Shadow Worlds

The first shadow world was the world from which my grandparents had emerged: the world of the East-European *shetl*, the small Jewish village. My grandparents were all dead before I had a chance to know them, so I had no link to traditional Jewish life. Neither my father nor mother ever related stories about that life that had been told to them by their parents. Perhaps these grandparents wanted to suppress their memories; but if this is true, then it is unusual, for my Jewish friends who had living grandparents were told such stories (generally about pogroms). Or perhaps the memory lapse, or the denial of memory was my parents' doing—too much remembering might compromise their project of guarded assimilation. But the shadow world of Eastern Europe was not entirely invisible. We used to go regularly to the Jewish cemetery to visit family graves. This was an extraordinary place of marble and granite, photographs of the dead under oval bronze covers, statuary and elaborate but ancient rickety wrought iron fences around the plots of immigrant burial societies, the societies and their members long dead. Very ancient men wandered about the cemetery, emaciated, with long discolored gray beards, dirty wide-brimmed black hats, and long dusty black coats which they never removed, even on the hottest of summer days. These men spoke to my parents in Yiddish, offering to say prayers for the dead for money. My parents always gave them money; a bit later one would hear them chanting and praying some distance from the graves. Another very ancient orthodox Jew, in the same disheveled costume and stained beard, would call upon my mother, carrying a can with Hebrew letters on it and a slot on top for coins. My mother always treated this man with great respect, giving money to his charity and a cup of tea to his clearly exhausted body, chatting a bit with him in Yiddish. My mother and father knew Yiddish, but always spoke English at home with a fair smattering of Yiddish words. It was bewildering to hear my mother speak this strange tongue to a figure who appeared to have emerged from the distant past. In spite of this strangeness, I knew that this language and these sick old men in black were somehow connected to me.

The other shadow world I took to be a real world, "the real America" I wanted to enter so desperately as a young woman. I knew it couldn't be found in Chicago or New York, where everyone was hyphenated, or black. (Now that the term "African-American" has come into use, they are hyphenated Americans too.) I imagined that the real America existed somewhere in the Midwest, in Iowa perhaps; it was a land of great civility and dignity, where people lived in big white frame houses with ancient trees on capacious lawns, a land of largely virtuous WASPS. It was, in a word, the land of Andy Hardy movies; it was Radioland, from whence issued serials such as Ma Perkins, which I listened to every day at lunch.[7] Ma was wise, sagacious, and serene, as was Andy Hardy's gray-haired, dignified father—the judge. This "place," the middle America of radio (I did much of my growing up before television) and the movies was clearly the center; we were on the margins. Urbana was full of somewhat more modest white frame houses with porches and trees that met overhead. On those mornings that I clattered down to church I wanted desperately to have a grandmother in one of those old white houses, a grandmother who, yes, baked cookies, a loving, serene, and wise soul with whom I could sit at dusk on the porch swing. I was eager to get into that world, to have parents who never raised their voices or lost their tempers, who would say to you, quietly and with dignity, if they were displeased, "Go to your room." No such words were ever spoken in my family. Disagreements descended almost immediately into quarrels and then into shouting matches, often into screaming matches in which everyone's dignity was lost. I usually ended up out of control, crying hysterically. Looking back on this, I cannot remember what these frequent quarrels were all about; I remember only the overheated atmosphere and the rapid departure on the part of my parents and myself from rationality. Two ideas clung to me at that period: "Jews are too materialistic," which was believed by Jews themselves as well as Gentiles and "Jews are loud." The latter claim, unlike the former, seemed, sadly, to be borne out by the decibel level of my home.

IV. A Return (More or Less) to Origins

Slowly, in fits and starts, and not without running down some blind alleys, I was able to construct an identity that was closer to my father's identity than it was to my youthful apostasy. Having read Sartre and Heidegger, I came to see that it was impossible to avoid "facticity," a sedimentation of facts that are true about one whether chosen or not—though one's facticity is always understood in the light of one's particular project of existence, i.e., the meaning one gave to existence through chosen aims and ambitions. I came to see that many of the things I thought about Jews were either false, or unobjectionable. While I thoroughly disliked the overheated emotional climate of my family, the stereotypical WASP stiff upper lip, suppression of emotion, and silence about what is really important, is perhaps even a poorer way to live. The charge of "materialism," leveled against Jews, is absurd. We thought that Jews were "too materialistic" only because most of the people we knew were Jews. The whole country, the culture of "late-stage" capitalism, encourages, indeed requires, high levels of consumption. In this, Jews are perhaps more like their neighbors than they are in any other way. As Jews tend to have a higher per capita income than most other Americans, perhaps we consume more, in which case the charge "materialistic" is just sour grapes.

For a time, I began to believe that Jews were *better* than other people. Weren't we, after all, over-represented in progressive circles, given our numbers in the population? Weren't more of us at least liberals, surprising given our relative affluence? Haven't Jews encouraged women's education when other groups did not? Weren't Reform and Conservative denominations quicker to ordain women than many other religious groups? Of the four men who are said to have influenced modern society the most—Darwin, Marx, Freud, and Einstein—weren't three of them Jews? Weren't Jews just smarter than other people? One could go on and on with this list, but one should not: Jewish chauvinism is no better than internalized anti-Semitism. If Jews have excelled in some areas, the reasons for this are quite complex and they are to be found in accidents of history and culture.[8] There is nothing intrinsically superior about Jews. I just wrote this, but do I believe it? I think I do, but only after many pendulum swings in the course of my adult life between pro- and anti-Semitism.

To speak now not just of Jewish chauvinism, but of Jewish triumphalism: I confess to having felt joy and pride not now, but in past Israeli military victories. Ever the romantic, I found irresistible the images of strong, bronzed Sabras sitting proudly atop their tanks as they rolled victorious through the desert. The sudden burst of pride not just I, but other Jews as well, felt all those years ago is a measure of how deeply and unconsciously entrenched in us is the stereotype of the Jew as coward, the Jew as victim, as "he who is to be slapped." We needed new images of who we were that did not shame us and we got them, in part, from Israel. But now, I am no supporter of Israeli foreign policy; I am appalled, as are many Jews and non-Jews, by Israel's treatment of the Palestinians. Like my father I hold the formerly unpopular but growing view among American Jews that the Palestinians should have their own state as was envisioned in the original United Nations partition plan. Israel is now just another nation-state, pursuing what it (perhaps mistakenly) believes is its own self-interest. I owe no political allegiance to Israel but I am fiercely attached to hope for its survival.

I feel comfortable now with my Jewish identity, having (I hope) steered a course between the Scylla of Jewish self-hatred and the Charbydis of Jewish triumphalism. I sometimes find myself attracted to dark-haired Jewish-looking men: the hegemony of the big blond jock is over. I never fail to observe the Seder, in spite of the death of my parents, either making one myself or managing to get invited somewhere. I mark the solemn day of atonement, Yom Kippur. I have just read my first Holocaust memoir, the superb *The Drowned and the Saved*, by Primo Levi. I celebrate Christmas as a pagan holiday marking the winter solstice. I have a Christmas tree.

I call the pattern of my identity formation "dialectical." There is a first moment in which my Jewish identity is no different from that of my parents. While I listened to countless "What is a Jew?" debates at home, they were for me abstract; my own identity was uninterrogated. In stage two I play with apostasy and, in Germany, passing. Finally, I return to a sense of self very like that of my parents, though with some significant differences. I lack my parents' gnawing suspicion that "deep down" all Gentiles are anti-Semitic. The differences between my parents' Jewish sense of self and my own stand out most clearly in their near-hysterical fear that I might marry outside the group. My parents were Yiddish speakers of immigrant parents who may have told them of the pogroms. They grew up in an America in which discrimination was overt, blatant, and legally allowable. When my father was twenty years old, one-third of the native-born white men in the neighboring state of Indiana were members of the Ku Klux Klan.[9] In a state with few African-Americans, the Klan leaders railed against the banks, the railroads, big business, Catholics, and Jews. The world in which I came of age was far different from theirs; anti-Semitism did not disappear but it ceased to be a prominent feature of the social landscape. I myself, except in Munich, never encountered it after childhood.

My father had a highly developed professional identity and also an American identity. While his Jewish identity was strong, it was also ambiguous and complex. It was already, as is mine, a synthesis of Jewish identity with the European cultural tradition whose art, literature, and philosophy (much of it influenced, often profoundly, by Christianity) is formative in the education of a Western secular intellectual. The condition, so discussed by postmodernists, of rifts and fissures where a "unified" self was supposed to be, did not come as news to me; it was just "the way we were" (and are). Unlike my father, I feel a strong connection to and an identification with a leftist political tradition not just in Europe, but in Mexico and here at home as well. My fantasy grandmother is no longer Ma Perkins but Emma Goldman.

V. Other Patterns of Jewish Identity

There are of course other ways of being Jewish in the United States today. I describe the answers to the question "What is a Jew?" of three persons known to me.[10] There is, first of all, the "virtual apostasy" of Carol. Her Jewishness is never mentioned but it is never denied either. Carol marries a Gentile and takes his Gentile name (though plenty of Jewish identified persons change their names). Carol never marks Jewish holidays or shows any interest at all in Jewish history or culture.

Then there is Aaron, formerly Arthur, an "anti-assimilationist." Coming from a background somewhat like my own, he concludes that our parents went too far in the direction of assimilation and that our lives have been impoverished as a result. Aaron wears a *yamulke* everywhere. A philosophy teacher like myself, he finds nothing interesting *but* Jewish history, culture, religion, and philosophy. He goes regularly to the synagogue and appears to have abandoned his earlier atheism for piety. He becomes so active in the synagogue that any possibility of participation in a "mixed" group—political or professional—is forgone. He looks long and hard for a Jewish woman whose identity construction is compatible with his own. He finds her. While Aaron and his wife practice birth control, in time, they have two children, both with Hebrew names, who are sent to Jewish day school. Aaron and his family celebrate all and only Jewish holidays. Ethnic Jewish dishes adorn his table. Influenced by the women's movement, Aaron and his wife share some domestic responsibilities. These include the keeping of a kosher kitchen, the responsibility for which, however, falls mainly on Aaron's wife.

Finally, Susan. Her pattern of identity formation I call "reclaiming the past for the present—and future." Susan rejects utterly her parents' atheism and their commitment to liberalism and feminism. She joins a Chassidic community and after a year or so goes permanently with those who converted her to Israel. Her life resembles in many ways the lives of my orthodox Jewish great-grandmothers in a Polish *shtetl* of the last century. The opportunity to spend her life in the study of Torah (the principal source of status in such communities) is denied her because of her sex. What Jewish education she gets is, in comparison, superficial; mostly, she is taught the proper duties of a Jewish wife and mother.[11] She accepts both the traditional division of labor and the subordination of women. In time, a marriage is arranged for her, though she retains veto power over the choice of a bridegroom. Her community does not sanction birth control; hence, Susan has three children before she is twenty-five. She goes regularly to the *mikva*, the ritual bath for women, where women purify themselves after menstrual periods and childbirth and before marriage. The state of Israel has given considerable autonomy in many legal matters to the ultra-Orthodox. While a religious divorce is not impossible, it is extremely difficult. If Susan should want a divorce and if a divorce were to be granted, she would lose custody of her children and, likely as not, she would have to leave the community. Hence if Susan wishes to return to the United States on a permanent basis, and her husband (also an American convert) does not, she would lose effective custody, or, in the case of divorce, legal custody of her children. Hence, her choice of identity, made in the period of typical identity crisis—late adolescence, early adulthood—will have far graver consequences for the future course of her life than did my own flirtation with Unitarianism.

VI. Some Existential Reflections

In the course of writing my autobiographical narrative—an exercise in remembering—I remembered the enjoinder to remember in the Haggadah: "It is incumbent upon every Israelite in every generation to imagine if he (sic) had actually gone out from Egypt." This raises the question whether one has a moral obligation to remember and preserve the history and folklore of one's people, a theme neglected in the standard literature of moral philosophy. It is against the pressure to assimilate, or to disappear entirely, that memory must be mobilized: without shared memory, group cohesion is lost; without cohesion the existence of the group is threatened. Forgetting—for Jews in particular—achieves the aim of our enemies: a world without Jews.

This raises three interesting questions: (a) What is the ground of the obligation to remember? (b) What is there in a group's ethnicity that deserves to be remembered and (c) What sorts of remembering and preserving behavior will satisfy the obligation to remember, if there is such an obligation?

In regard to (a) above: Since we are not human atoms, our own identities are lodged, in part, in group identities. To forget who we are and from whence we have come, then, is tantamount to losing a part of ourselves. Without an anchor, we may become deracinated, alienated and forlorn, homeless, belonging nowhere. This assumes that the dominant culture cannot supply satisfactory substitutes (can it?) and accounts, perhaps, for the tenacity with which people—even people such as Aaron and Susan, far removed in time and space from the mother culture—reach out to older ethnic identities. But insofar as somewhat assimilated American Jews have a complex identity, there are, as I suggested earlier in regard to the history of domestic and international radical agitation, other identity-creating resources.

Another argument for ethnic preservation points to the richness and complexity of multi-ethnic societies: ethnicity as a source of largely aesthetic and sensory pleasures. But does this obligate every "ethnic" to periodically wear the folk-costumes of his or her mother culture, eat its foods, dance its folk-dances? It seems to me that there is no such obligation; nevertheless, ethnic identification as a counterweight to alienation and this identification as an occasion for the inclusion of one's cultural origin in the panoply of human diversity seem to me to be good reasons for memory and preservation.

But there are substantial counterarguments to these "good reasons" as well. Ethnic pride often fosters group narcissism; the group positions itself as the one and all others as "other." This positioning regularly takes the form of an assertion of superiority: human cultures and subcultures are constructed as a hierarchy with one's own group at or near the top; all thought of human solidarity and not just the difference, but the commonality of human interests flies out the window. Hence, ethnic pride appears as the flip side of contempt for the other. Furthermore, the whole effort appears to be an exercise in bad faith: the superiority of one's cultural tradition, as Sartre would say, is based on unpersuasive evidence. Mediocre folk cultures, for example, are greatly inflated in value. The sufferings of one's group are seen as more real and pressing (and most human groups have suffered at some time or another) than the sufferings of others. This can lead to the denial or willful ignorance of the suffering of others. Over-investment in ethnicity can be a cause as well as an effect of aggression, also of paranoia: "The others are taking or plan to take what is rightfully ours." It can also be an alibi for grabbing land or other resources from those whose very ethnic presence in the midst of the aggressors threatens the purity of *their* ethnicity. The recent history of the former Yugoslavia, I think, bears out much of what I have said.

These arguments may fit some groups, but when we consider groups that have been targeted for extermination (e.g., Jews, gypsies, homosexuals) the issue becomes more complex. Insofar as I will the perpetuation of the group, I have an obligation to help to perpetuate it, though of course the question as to what is "proper" perpetuation leads back to the unanswerable question, "What is a Jew?" In regard to (a) above, I do not see how to ground this obligation in Kantian universalism or in consequentialist considerations. The Haggadah does not address its injunction to remember to all rational beings, but to "Israelites." In reply to (b) above, neither the intrinsic values and accomplishments of the group—its literature, food, folklore, religion—grounds my obligation. I may be indifferent to all this, preferring to devote myself to what I see as pressing ecological concerns that affect the survival of all races, religions, nations, and ethnicities. Furthermore there are other cultural traditions that may "deserve" memory and preservation as well. Add to this the consideration that preservation is perhaps best accomplished by specialists— linguists, historians, anthropologists. The primordial question is much simpler: do I will a world without Jews? I would not know where to look for further grounding: these are my people and I will their survival. This is a special obligation best understood in the framework of existentialist ethics. My obligation obliges because I choose to be obligated by it. This is not to say that *only* Jews have an obligation to remember, say, the Holocaust, or the rich folk culture of East European Jewry.

Finally, to return briefly to the question of what behaviors are required to discharge such an obligation: For Aaron and Susan, refusal to attend religious services is a crime against remembering at best, a crime against God, at worst. So is marrying outside the group. It is often said that the greatest threat to the survival of American Jews is our high rate of intermarriage (estimated by some at 50 percent). Perhaps Sartre is right: group cohesion feeds on persecution from without.[12]

There are many remembering behaviors. Here is a sample: reading and discussing Jewish history; learning to make a matzoh ball that floats on air; standing in solidarity with Jews everywhere who are persecuted and with the Israelis when they are in the right; going to synagogue on Yom Kippur even if one is a non-believer to hear the great (and, I think, the only) credo of Jewish religious doctrine: "Hear O Israel, the Lord Our God, the Lord is One."

There is sufficient demand, so I understand, to support the teaching of Yiddish at Northwestern University.[13] The same generation that demanded the teaching of Yiddishkeit has rediscovered the klezmer band, the lively small folk band of East European Jewry that had, in the nineteenth and early twentieth centuries, a wide audience both in Eastern Europe and in immigrant enclaves here. Such bands have proliferated in the United States and are often heard on programs that feature more familiar folk music. The lead singer of the Maxwell Street Klezmer Band, one of the best, has learned Yiddish in order to give authenticity to her performances. This woman and her band surely remember and preserve.

Whoever visits the Holocaust Museum in Washington, D.C., is given a card that carries the name and some little information about a Holocaust victim. The card bears witness to the fact that this individual lived on earth, had his or her share of the joys and disappointments of life, a name, and a history. The card one carries throughout the visit bears witness to the uniqueness and irreplaceability of this person: an attempt, of necessity feeble, to annul the frightful anonymity of mass murder.

This list could be expanded indefinitely. But thinking about this list, constructed haphazardly and without system, indeed, thinking of the multitude of behaviors that might well turn up on such a list, I have a deep sense of unease: I realize that I have done very little myself to discharge the obligation I feel toward remembering and preserving my Jewish heritage. The trajectory of this chapter has led me to realize that the obligation I feel is somewhat at odds with the way I have lived.

While I can, indeed, make matzoh balls that float on air, I have married twice, both times to non-Jews. Charles Mills, argues in "Do Black Men Have a Duty to Marry Black Women?" that the frequency with which successful black men marry white women may well represent the internalization of racist stereotypes of beauty and worth that are ubiquitous in a racist system such as ours. An acceptance of racist criteria (the wife's white status will somehow raise his) will not only reveal the black's man's continuing lack of self-respect, but it robs the black woman not only of a share in the black man's prosperity but also of the homage due to her beauty and desirability.[14] Hence, the baleful message conveyed by the choice of a white wife perpetuates the racist positioning of the black woman that puts her at the very bottom of the social pyramid.

While the situations of blacks and Jews are very different might it be possible that something similar has been going on with me—an unconscious desire to soar over tribal barriers to the greater prestige of the Gentile world? I do not believe that this is so[15] but can I be certain? Mainstream moral philosophy typically assumes a transparency on the part of the ethical subject as to her motives or (as in the case of Plato) it holds out the promise of such a transparency. When I consider how much of our behavior is unconsciously motivated, especially in matters of sex and love, much canonical moral philosophy seems to me to be at best irrelevant, at worst naive.

Nor have I had children. If I had, I would have raised them as Jews (i.e., consonant with what we know about children's need to rebel). I would have tried to influence them to accept a Jewish identity and to learn something about the richness and diversity of Jewish culture—but I never had children. In light of the fate of Jews in this century, did I—do other Jewish women (and men)—have a very special duty to increase and multiply? As things stand now, I will not even replace myself in the United States Census.

Some closing remarks: I recognize an obligation to my ethnicity that moral philosophy cannot justify rationally. I recognize too the necessity of picking and choosing among an indefinite number of identificatory behaviors. So when it comes to the actual discharge of my obligation, I am on my own again. Where do I go for guidance in deciding how to balance this obligation against other obligations—to my students, my intimates, my community, my commitment to struggle against racism, militarism, sexism, and pollution? Sartre tells us that the choice of a moral authority is already a decision about what sort of advice one is willing to accept. I live as I suppose most people live, in confusion, recognizing obligations but rarely doing what is necessary to discharge them, often not knowing how exactly to discharge them at all, in a kind of moral fog, lurching here and blundering there. How much we have given to moral philosophy— how many hours when others slept, poring over tomes that were often difficult in the extreme—and how little it has given us in return!

Notes

This chapter was previously published in *Marginal Groups and Mainstream American Culture*, edited by Yolanda Estes et al. (Lawrence: University Press of Kansas, 2000).

1. This is a long thank-you list of things God did for the Israelites, assuring Him that if he had done x, but not y, "it would have been sufficient"—"*dyanu*" in Hebrew.

2. *Passover Haggadah with Music* (New York: Hebrew Publishing Co., 1912), 29.

3. Of course, interpretations vary widely. More religious Jews see in the story of the Exodus evidence of God's special relationship with the Jewish people.

4. "Losers" because it was considered a disgrace for a middle-class woman unless she was single (and to be single was to have lost big. An "old maid" was a fate worse than death) to have to work for wages. This was a sign of the husband's failure to provide for his family—a misfortune and disgrace.

5. Perhaps. Or perhaps it stems from an incompletely resolved Oedipus Complex; anyone who looked like my dark-haired father would set off unconscious oedipal anxiety. Or does it stem from the fact that my mother was blond as a child and bore a child, my brother, with a beautiful head of curly blond hair? A blond Jewish baby! Friends and relatives came to marvel at this miracle child, especially at his hair; five years older and a brunette, I was (briefly) ignored.

6. Seeing me carrying a book about the Rosenbergs, my German landlord in Munich said, "Of course they did it for money." "No," I answered, "I don't think they got any money; anyhow, I think they did it out of ideological commitment." "Impossible," he answered, "they were Jews so they must have done it for the money."

7. The *locus classicus* of this kind of Jewish longing for the center is to be found in Philip Roth's unjustly maligned *Portnoy's Complaint* (New York: Vintage Books, 1994). I read parts of this book with the sense that I was reading my own biography. I understand now that "Radioland" and the TV sitcom culture that succeeded it were the products of an entertainment industry. There is substantial confusion between life and art: fictional families (*Father Knows Best*) are now part of the "family values" ideology of the political right.

8. In Eastern Europe, from which most American Jews emigrated, it was illegal for a Jew to own land. As agriculture was the principal source of wealth, Jews were forced to learn crafts, to become petty traders or money-lenders. Moreover, it was a religious duty for a male Jew to be literate and to study the Torah and if possible, the voluminous commentary that had grown up around the first five books of Moses. The community subsidized academically promising young men.

9. M. William Lutholtz, *Grand Dragon: D. C. Stephenson and the Ku Klux Klan in Indiana* (West Lafayette, Ind.: Purdue University Press, 1991), 55.

10. These are real people; I have changed their names to protect their privacy. I am not passing judgment on their stories.

11. Tamar El-Or, *Educated and Ignorant: Ultraorthodox Jewish Women and Their World* (Boulder and London: Lynne Rienner Publishers, 1994).

12. Jean-Paul Sartre, *Anti-Semite and Jew* (New York: Schocken Books Inc., 1948).

13. Oral communication from Northwestern University professor Irwin Weil.

14. Charles Mills, "Do Black Men Have a Duty to Marry Black Women?" in *Rethinking Masculinity: Philosophical Explorations in Light of Feminism*, May, Strikwerda, and Hopkins, eds. (New York: Rowman & Littlefield, 1996).

15. Neither man gave me entree into a higher social status. It might be argued, in the case of at least one of them, that since I was middle class and he working class, I raised his status. See note 5.

CHAPTER SEVEN

~

In Defense of Guilt

"Bleeding heart liberal!" "Guilty liberal!" Two terms of opprobrium, one thrown out by the American Right, the other by the Left. I shall try to show that both charges, although from opposing political perspectives, are embedded in a series of masculinist polarities. Revisiting guilt points up the difficulties, whatever our politics, of escaping from the pervasiveness of sexist conceptual frameworks.

The term, "bleeding heart liberal," is typically uttered with scorn, not so much by right-wing politicians as by the *enragees* who elect them. One hears this phrase often, especially on right-wing talk radio, virtually the only talk radio on the U.S. airwaves. "Liberal" is the ultimate term of opprobrium in these right-wing times since a domestic "radical" is virtually unimaginable. Thus, "bleeding heart liberal" has become consummate abuse.

Now this has always perplexed me: why isn't it a good thing, a praiseworthy thing, to have a bleeding heart? Normally, no one, not even a liberal would have a heart that bled for Bill Gates.[1] Those for whom the bleeding hearts bleed are the less fortunate. Why, then, is such scorn heaped upon those who feel compassion for them? Isn't compassion a virtue? What would a world without compassion be like? Isn't it better to have a compassionate heart than a cold, cold heart? I am further perplexed by the fact that many of those who excoriate "bleeding heart liberals" belong to the Christian Right, a congeries of organizations that regard the United States as a Christian, or (in their less anti-Semitic and more "multicultural" moods) a "Judeo-Christian," country. Now Jesus Christ and the Virgin Mary are often pictured with hearts emanating divine rays or with hearts that bleed; often-times their hearts emanate divine rays *and* they bleed. So "bleeding heart" is consummate abuse in the mouths of the very people who worship members of a holy family with hearts that bleed. How can this be? How can the poli-tics of the Christian Right stand in such sharp contradiction to the religious iconography of traditional Christianity? "A foolish consistency may be the hobgoblin of little minds," as Emerson once said, but this is taking inconsis-tency too far. Jesus is all right as a deity, but you wouldn't want him making policy; you hope the Virgin will plead your case before God, but you wouldn't elect her to Congress.

The compassion of bleeding hearts, they tell us, is corrosive, for bleeding hearts refuse to cut the poor off welfare, and welfare creates dependency. We rob the poor of their initiative when we provide them with a "safety net." The bleeding hearts are too "permissive": what we need is "tough love." Here, clearly, is a gendered subtext of tender and tough, permissive and dis-ciplinary, dove and hawk: the first term suggests the feminine, the second the masculine. The bald eagle that represents our country is a predator; the Par-aclete is a dove. Jesus and the Virgin Mary, the effeminate and the feminine, indeed all the bleeding hearts are soft; neocons (neoconservatives) are hard.

Most of us always thought that poverty came first, then welfare; but George Gilder et al. want us to believe that welfare creates poverty![2] Wel-fare rewards the lazy and shiftless; take it away and they will develop the work ethic—or starve. Never mind that the majority of persons on welfare are children, or that the average recipient spends two years on welfare, not a lifetime. Never mind that single mothers are disproportionately repre-sented on the welfare rolls: their dependency, so it is said, stems from "lib-eral do-gooders," not from women's historic low wages, or from the scarcity and when available, the expense of decent daycare. Never mind that life on the minimum wage will not lift a family above the poverty line and if it should, goodbye perhaps to Medicaid and food stamps—holdovers from the "War on Poverty" that has been supplanted, so it seems, by a war on the poor. Never mind that "downsizing" has impoverished whole communities or that hundreds of thousands of jobs, both skilled and unskilled, have been automated out of existence or else exported to low wage Third World coun-tries whose governments are only too glad to guarantee, often by repression and torture, "stability."

I turn now to another liberal persona, this time an object of contempt not for the Right, but for the Left—the "guilty liberal."[3] In the political culture I sought out in the late 1960s as the limitations of liberalism became more and more apparent to me, no one, not even hard-bitten reactionaries, was regarded with more contempt than "guilty liberals." (This made me very un-comfortable because, prior to my embrace of radicalism, I had been a liberal for many years and I knew in my secret heart that I was, well, guilty.) So who were these pariahs? They were well-meaning folk who were pricked by con-science—"liberal guilt"—in the face of clear injustice, but who made merely token gestures (like paying the black cleaning lady a few dollars more) and who were unwilling to forgo privilege (all liberals were assumed to be privi-leged) in order to make the kinds of sacrifices that social revolution was sup-posed to require. Since they were not prepared to make sacrifices, when "push came to shove" liberals would just disappear or even go over to the other side. Hence, they were untrustworthy, fickle. These guilty liberals were, in other words, hypocrites and cowards.

But have we not seen some strange departures from principle on the part of notable radicals? Rennie Davis (of the Chicago Seven), dropped out and became a disciple of the thirteen-year-old Perfect Master (a leading guru of the day); Jerry Rubin (also one of the Chicago Seven) a Wall Street broker; Eldridge Cleaver, a born-again Christian and shill for American mega-corporations. Nor is it the case that liberals never stand on principle when the going gets rough, or even sacrifice for it. Thousands of white Northern-ers, many liberals among them, went South as volunteers during the Civil Rights movement. They went with no guarantee that they would return; in-deed, some did not return.

Another ground of condemnation of liberal guilt is associated with the be-lief that guilt is not a proper motivator of political action, because an emo-tion can never take the place of a correct analysis. The construction of such an analysis is not typically believed to spring from any particular emotion. This idea is thoroughly Cartesian: emotion is at best superfluous, at worst, a snare that can lead us to incorrect conclusions. Cognition trumps emotion, once again. Radicals, we believed, have a tough and complex analysis—a class analysis accompanied perhaps by considerations of gender or race. Rad-icals permit themselves certain emotions, to be sure—outrage at the action of right-wing dictators, joy at the prospect of the triumph of socialism. We did not permit ourselves guilt. Guilt was for liberals. Liberals had only a few woolly minded ideas about the efficacy of electoral politics, "bourgeois right," and—guilt, an unclean emotion in which, like self-pity, some are thought to wallow. Also, liberals were typically regarded as fickle: just when you think they are on your side, they disappear, or temporize.

The gendered subtext is a bit harder to see here than it was in the case of the "bleeding heart liberal," but it is visible, nonetheless. On the one hand, tough-minded, hard-edged, even "scientific" analysis, courage, and the readiness to sacrifice; on the other, woolly minded political theory that shrinks from the implications of its political values—namely, that the achievement of genuine liberty and true equality will require an overthrow of the existing order—hence intellectual cowardice, but also personal cowardice, fickleness, and unclean emotions like guilt. It cannot escape attention that the qualities ascribed to liberals by both their right-wing and left-wing critics are those traditionally associated in our culture with women and "the feminine."

"Let's Hear It for Guilt"

In the balance of this chapter, I take a thread from the preceding discussion and follow it out. I shall argue, against the conviction of the American Left, that guilt can be one among many acceptable motivations for political action. I shall argue too that although the standard characterizations of guilt in the literature of moral psychology are not inaccurate, they are simplistic and somewhat shallow when examined in a political context. It should be clear in what follows that the political action in question is action taken on behalf of others less fortunate than oneself.

I want to specify at the outset the uses and forms of guilt (there are many) that I shall *not* be discussing. First, guilt used as a weapon, usually by one person against another, a practice known colloquially as "guilt-tripping." This can be extremely damaging not just in personal relationships, but in political organizations as well, especially women's organizations. This is a big topic, and I shall save it for another time. A second form of guilt I shall not be discussing (and possibly the cause of the phobic reaction of my comrades to any discussion of guilt) is the unconscious guilt, left over from childhood, that can manifest itself in neurotic symptoms. The same people who oversaw my radicalization were or had been heavy consumers of psychotherapeutic services (myself included); among the more favored members of the middle class, "going into therapy" was (and probably still is) the most common way of dealing with emotional crises and/or pervasive unhappiness. The kinds of guilt we were encouraged to recognize and to try to purge in therapy were thought to stem from tabooed infantile erotic and aggressive desires.

Guilt by Complicity

In the analytic tradition of moral psychology, guilt is a subjective experience of self-assessment called forth by the violation of principles which a person values and by which she feels herself bound.[4] It is not necessary to have violated such principles oneself; one can be guilty of complicity with those who have, e.g., one's government. There is required for complicity (1) the knowledge that certain deeds have been done; (2) the recognition that these deeds violate principles which one values and by which one feels oneself bound; and (3) the knowledge that one has so far done nothing to make the doers of unprincipled behavior cease their violation of moral and/or legal norms. Now, the United States government has violated many principles which I value—principles of international law and of common human decency. What this government does, it does in my name, by my elected representatives, with my tax money, so to speak, over my signature. All of this makes me, as long as I acquiesce, an accomplice in the crimes of my government: I am guilty of complicity.[5]

Now everyone knows that the U.S. government is largely an instrument of the concentrations of capital that have bought the White House and the Congress. I say "largely," not "entirely," because some resistance to the government and its actions is still possible. Government is a site of contestation, even though the corrosive effects of mega-corporationism have brought it about that the contest is always between David and Goliath. What happens at the grass roots does sometimes matter. Even though some people have been sacrificed, martyred (the Black Panthers), it is often possible in the United States today for a person to be politically effective (of course in concert with others) without running much risk of imprisonment, loss of employment, or death. This makes continued complicity in the crimes of the government especially reprehensible.

The landmark Civil Rights Bill of 1964 was passed after seven years of intense political agitation. The war in Vietnam might have dragged on forever if not for mass dissent and mass mobilization. Agitation led to the cutoff of funding for the Contra War: avenues for funding had to be found illegally. Similarly, the women's movement has made the mistreatment of women in every area of life visible to millions of people; in response to this (a response that has been feeble, but detectable), government has granted rights and enacted remedial measures in areas to which it was heretofore oblivious.

The recognition that one is guilty of complicity is not incompatible with righteous indignation or with feelings of solidarity with the victims of injustice, the latter two "respectable" motivations for the "correct" radical.

Guilt by Virtue of Privilege

An awareness of the guilt of complicity can be called forth by specific acts or policies of my government. But government is only one institution in the social totality in which we discover our enjoyment of privilege or our exclusion from it. The guilt of the privileged is not attached to any particular act or policy; guilt of this sort is occasioned by something far more global, namely,

the very structure of the social totality itself, that positions some as privileged, others as "underprivileged." These positions are determined largely,
but not always irrevocably, by the accidents of birth. The guilt people sometimes experience in the recognition of complicity with government is generally occasioned by specific events, e.g., the CIA's involvement in the overthrow of a legally elected president or an imperialist military intervention.
But the social totality that produces privilege (and hence the guilt of the
privileged) need do nothing out of the ordinary. It needs only to continue to
function *normally*. Joseph K., in Kafka's *The Trial*, is arrested "in a country
with a legal constitution, there was universal peace, all the laws were in
force."[6] Seeing the social world we inhabit as normal, generally lawful, rest-
ing on the consent of the governed, etc., makes it more difficult (especially
if we are its beneficiaries) to see the ways in which, even though "all the laws
were in force," it is also a complex network of systemic injustices.

"Privilege" in this context is a special advantage, or favor that is granted
to some individual or group of individuals and not to others; the term also
carries the connotation of an exemption from some duty or burden. The
guilt that emerges from my recognition that I occupy a privileged position
in the social totality has to do not only with the benefits I enjoy that I have
not earned but also and equally with the fact that others have been excluded
from their enjoyment unjustly by a mere accident of birth. Here is a double
consciousness: the recognition of my unearned privilege and the concomitant recognition that the unjust denial of privilege to others is the result of
the "normal" workings of the social order. In my own case, the unearned
privileges I enjoy are white-skin privilege, class privilege, and heterosexual
privilege. Now, it is often the case that one is privileged in some ways and
disadvantaged in others. As a woman, for example, I am denied phallic privilege, though this denial is usually (but not always) tempered by the fact
that I am heterosexual, that I have a decent income, a steady job, and that
I do not suffer the additional disadvantages that accrue to women of color
and lesbians.

Let us consider first the question of earned and unearned privilege. If our
society were a perfect meritocracy, what appears to be a gross maldistribution
of social goods would be a rationale that some would argue is just. People
would get what they earned—no more and no less. Conservatives like to pre-
tend that our society is sufficiently meritocratic to justify the uneven distri-
bution of money and power. They are fond of pointing to the disadvantaged
backgrounds of specific individuals (e.g., President Clinton) who pulled
themselves up by their bootstraps and thus earned the privileges they enjoy.
True, there is, for many individuals, a connection between hard work, com-

mitment, sacrifice, and success. Conservatives have played compellingly on this connection. But no matter how hard a poor black boy from Arkansas might have struggled to improve his lot (as Clinton struggled to improve his), it is highly unlikely that this black boy could have been elected president. At any rate, the true test of the justice of social arrangements is not whether they allow, from time to time, extraordinary individuals with extraordinary abilities to rise to the top, but how well the system as a whole works for ordinary people.

The idea of meritocracy is tied logically to the image of society as a contest. Now a fair contest requires a "level playing field," i.e., an original situation in which the competitors begin at roughly the same place with the same or with comparable qualities. But the majority of advantaged individuals never shared a level playing field with their disadvantaged competitors. I take myself again as an example. I worked very hard and very long to climb the academic ladder, faced what was for me the sheer terror of Ph.D. examinations, agonized over a writer's block that delayed the writing of my dissertation, suffered terribly during the dreadful probationary period, published barely enough to get tenure, and, generally, had a psychology that combined substantial ambition with pervasive feelings of inadequacy and with fears both of failure and of success. Yet there were also factors quite beyond my control that helped me all along the way: my skin color, associated culturally more with intelligence than are the skin colors of others; a failure of female socialization that had made me into a marriage resister, shrinking in something like horror at the destiny to which most young women of my class and background aspired in those days—suburban housewifery; an intellectual father who made me his intellectual companion; philosophical discussions with my father who would sometimes change sides, just to give me practice; a house full of books, a community that valued education, even for women; no pressure from my parents to marry and have children; complete financial support from home through an undergraduate degree, which, while it was "only" at the state university (all my parents could afford) freed me from the necessity of getting even a campus job to study and allowed me to spar over endless cups of coffee with other young wannabe intellectuals about music, art, and the "big ideas." When I developed psychosomatic illnesses due to the stresses of graduate school and the later probationary period prior to the granting of tenure, my parents paid for me to see specialists not available through the student health plan.[7]

The very idea of society generally or the job market, particularly, as a level playing field is an ideological mystification that flies in the face of everything we know about the complex relationships of individuals to their communities and families, their schools, their parents' income level, their educational histories, temperaments, and psychologies. Alison Jaggar argues in *Feminist Politics and Human Nature* that the liberal values of freedom and equality (as long as "equality" carries with it the idea of competition on that level playing field) are in conflict, thus making liberal political theory itself incoherent. The only way to secure a level playing field would be to take children from their parents at birth and educate them identically in identical environments. This is unworkable in the current political climate, as it would incur astronomical expense. (The same politicos who maunder on about our no longer needing affirmative action because that level playing field is now a reality will not even appropriate sufficient funds to keep the worst of our scandalously unequal schools from collapsing, sometimes on the very heads of their students.) To level the playing field, anything more than token contact with parents would have to be denied, as would many preferences, say for toys or books, of children themselves. These intrusions into the family, flawed as the institution may be, deny very basic rights. It surprises me that so few people who call for a level playing field have thought through the implications of creating one. The nightmare scenario of massive state intervention cannot help but be implicated in any political perspective that imagines even modest success in life to be the earned consequence of a fair contest: the conditions required to make such a contest fair are repugnant.[8]

I am not suggesting that competitors in all contests be physically and mentally identical, which is, of course, impossible. Some contests select for certain traits in their winners (like height in basketball). But the great contest of life in this capitalist system also selects for certain advantages in *its* winners: these advantages are simultaneously the goods that it takes to come out on top, and the prizes waiting at the finish line, such goods as money and connections. This is indeed a vicious circularity.

The conservative view of society as a meritocracy not only denies the real effects of race, class, gender, sexual orientation, as these are played out in the lives of ordinary people, it very conveniently saddles the victims of these systemic biases with responsibility for their effects. Thus, poor people are poor because of a deficiency of personal responsibility, or the lack of a work ethic, because they are promiscuous or are socialized into a defective culture of poverty. There is merit in none of these charges. The same politicians who appear to agonize over the alleged lack of personal responsibility on the part of the poor seem sublimely unconcerned with their own personal responsibility for ridding this rich nation of its persistent poverty. It is not accidental that there is a large overlap between poverty and race. Widespread bigotry, one among many causes of poverty, can easily incorporate poverty into its racist view of the world: a marriage made in hell. In point of fact, most of the poor in this country are children; most welfare recipients are white.

If guilt by virtue of privilege fits the standard view of guilt in moral psychology, then the enjoyment of privilege must involve the violation of a moral principle. Here is a candidate for such a principle: it is wrong to enjoy privileges from which other people have been unjustly excluded, especially if one's privileges have been predicated upon the unjust exclusion of others. We examined above one kind of thinking that would make the excluded responsible for their own exclusion, thus canceling the "unjust" before "excluded." But there is another strategy also at work to exonerate the system and those it advantages. What if the disadvantaged are not just morally, but biologically unfit? Biological explanations for inequality abound. The newspapers seize on any study that purports to prove that there are biological differences between men and women that account for their social disparities, even while they (the popular press) ignore the mountain of studies that point to differential treatment of the sexes in virtually every domain. A few academics with respectable credentials seem unable to abandon the idea that blacks are genetically inferior to whites in regard to intelligence.[9] The "findings" are announced periodically to the reading public with some fanfare on the Right; in centrist publications such as the *New York Times*, the seriousness with which these claims are taken, even when they are (often hesitantly) rejected, grant these "scientific" studies a respectability they do not merit. I cannot review this debate here, which is, by now, centuries old.[10]

For the sake of argument, let us assume that findings of racial and gender inferiority are at least superficially plausible. Still, the racial and sexual differences these studies purport to uncover are generally quite slight; hence, if there are genetic differences between races or sexes, it is plausible that changes in childhood socialization could wipe them out altogether. In a speech lambasting *The Bell Curve*, the latest best seller which purports to demonstrate the inferiority of African-Americans in regard to intelligence, Stephen Jay Gould of Harvard demonstrated this quite dramatically. Taking off his glasses, he said, "I am myopic. My myopia is genetically determined." Letting this sink in for a bit, he put his glasses back on with a flourish. "Now," he said, "what has happened to my myopia?" But this gesture is hardly Gould's last word on the subject: he rejects unconditionally both the methodology and the conclusions of *The Bell Curve*.[11] Unfortunately, however, it is likely that most privileged people believe one or the other (or both) of the twin pillars of institutional privilege: the alleged biological and the alleged moral inadequacy of the un- and underprivileged.[12]

So far, my analysis suggests that privileged people in general are not innocent of injustice; nevertheless, only a fraction recognize this to be the case.
There is a striking encounter in Sartre's *Dirty Hands* that can perhaps teach
us something about the recognition—or the non-recognition—of responsibility. The play is set in a Balkan country in the closing days of World War
II. Hugo, the son of a wealthy industrialist, has joined the Proletarian Party.
George and Slick, two working-class members of the party, resent Hugo's
class privilege—his fine clothes, his trophy wife—and have been taunting
him. He joined the Party, they think "because it was the thing to do"; they
joined out of brute necessity, out of hunger. Finally Hugo bursts out angrily,

> For once you're right, my friend. I don't know what appetite is. If you could have seen
> the tonics they gave me as a kid; I always left half—what waste! Then they opened
> my mouth and told me: "One spoonful for Papa, one spoonful for Mamma" . . . and
> they pushed the spoon down my throat. . . . Then they had me drink blood fresh
> from the slaughterhouse, because I was pale; after that I never touched meat. My
> father would say every night: "This child has no appetite." Every evening he would
> say: "Eat, Hugo eat. You'll be sick." They had me take cod-liver oil; that's the
> height of luxury, medicine to make you hungry while others in the street would sell
> their souls for a beefsteak. I saw them pass under my window with their placards:
> "Give us bread." And then I would sit down at the table. "Eat, Hugo, eat." A spoon-
> ful for the night watchman who is on strike, a spoonful for the old woman who
> picks the parings out of the garbage can, a spoonful for the family of the carpenter
> who broke his leg. I left home. I joined the party, only to hear the same old song:
> "You've never been hungry, Hugo, what are you messing around here for? What can
> you know? You've never been hungry." Very well, then! I have never been hungry.
> Never! Never! Never! Now perhaps you can tell me what I can do to make you stop
> throwing it up to me.[13]

The taunting doesn't stop. Finally, Hoederer, the Party leader, intervenes on
Hugo's behalf: "You heard him? Come on now, tell him. Tell him what he has
to do, Slick, what do you want of him? Do you want him to cut off a hand? Or
tear out one of his eyes? . . . The hunger of others is not so easy to bear, either." One of the men says, "There's plenty who manage to put up with it very
nicely." And Hoederer replies, "That's because they have no imagination."[14]
     In Illyria, Sartre's mythical country, the social order is so skewed that some
children are stuffed to the point of nausea while others are starving. The con-
trast between the more privileged classes and the underclass in our own
country is not quite so grim. Nevertheless, the abject poverty of the homeless and the hopelessness and destitution of the urban black underclass in the
United States mirror the hunger of Illyria. Even though Hugo is a child, he

is able to imagine the misery of the population, this in a very literal sense: he carries in his mind images of the poor—the old woman who picks parings out of the garbage, the destitute family of the injured carpenter who cannot work. How do these images get into Hugo's head? Perhaps he has seen old women picking parings out of the garbage, perhaps not; but certainly he has seen the strikers in front of his father's house, carrying signs that say "Give Us Bread."

Hoederer is right: we need to imagine, in the most vivid sense, what it would be like to be one of the insulted and injured of this world, for the insults and injuries of others, when we open ourselves up to them as best we can, are indeed, not easy to bear. But for Hugo adequately to grasp the wrongness of his privilege, he needs more than imagination: he needs to unmask the moralizing or the Social Darwinist mystifications that regularly justify unredeemed human misery. Like most emotions, guilt, when it is acknowledged as a judgment of self, has an affective dimension which is inextricable from a cognitive dimension (in this case, rejections of the kinds of rationalizations for poverty that are pervasive in bourgeois society).

What I have called "guilt by reason of privilege" is now revealed as a variant of "guilt by reason of complicity." Hugo recognizes his complicity in an unjust social order, indeed the complicity of his *class*. The two kinds of guilt differ in regard to their objects: acts and policies of government in the one, the structure of an entire social totality in the other.

Of course a social totality does not spring into being from nowhere; its character has been slowly and steadily formed precisely by human actions and government policies sedimented over time. But in addition, there are historical and psychological factors that have played an important role as well. Moreover, the social totality is riven by contradictions, and it is always in process of change. Guilt by reason of privilege is more interesting theoretically than simple guilt by complicity, just because its object is difficult, perhaps impossible, to grasp fully. Terms like "social totality" or "the established order" fall easily enough onto the page, but their referents contain regions of confusion and opacity.

Most human beings do not want to feel that they are in any way guilty of perpetuating human misery. This is undoubtedly the reason that my white middle-class students respond regularly with anger, defensiveness, or denial when I suggest to them that we whites enjoy privileges that are systematically denied to non-whites. "I've never abused or insulted a black person!" or "My parents came here thirty years ago from Croatia: my forebears were peasants, not slaveholders." My students are onto something, namely, the normal distinction between having done something wrong and having done nothing wrong. I am making the counter-intuitive claims that one can be guilty *without having done anything wrong* and that one can be guilty without feeling guilty. I am guilty by virtue of my relationship to wrongdoing, a relationship that I did not create but have not severed, either.

Thus, the standard characterization of guilt in moral psychology is too "psychologistic." On my view, I am guilty by virtue of simply being who and what I am: a white woman, born into an aspiring middle-class family in a racist and class-ridden society. The existentialists were fond of saying that guilt was endemic to the human condition: I confess to never having fully understood this until now. The recognition of unearned privilege does not necessarily or inevitably engender guilt feelings in the heart of the one privileged. The response might well be anger, or dismay. But if a person feels guilty because her or his location in the social totality has been a source of unearned privilege, then, in my view, that person is, so to speak, "entitled" to her guilt. There is complicity involved in this second kind of guilt, just as there is in the first, i.e., in the recognition that I am implicated in, for example, my government's violation of international law. My role in the maintenance of an unjust social order is a fact, *whether I recognize it or not*. Guilt, then, need not be felt as emotions are typically felt: it is an existential-moral condition that can be, but need not be accompanied by "feeling guilty."

A Note on White-Skin Privilege

When Hoederer in Sartre's *Dirty Hands*, tells George and Slick that the hunger of others is hard to bear, they reply, quite rightly, that "There's plenty who manage to put up with it very nicely." How is it that so many respectable, even pious persons do manage to "put up with it very nicely"? In my view, this is one of the most important and still unanswered questions in political theory. In addition to the role played by the ideological mystifications of "personal responsibility" and Social Darwinism, there is the standard reply: Most people will struggle, even to the point of taking up arms, to maintain their privilege.[15] Their resolution is grounded not only in self-interest and self-serving ideologies, but, for some persons, in a number of complex psychological factors that I have analyzed elsewhere.[16] There is also self-deception and morally culpable ignorance on a large scale. The more fortunate perceive few links between their own privilege and the misery of the underprivileged. The two are perceived as entirely unconnected. The radical friends of my youth were right when they emphasized the necessity for an analysis—one that links these phenomena. Moreover, much privilege, be it white-skin privilege, phallic, class, or hetero-normative privilege, although substantial and pervasive, is also *imperceptible*.

Peggy McIntosh, associate director of the Center for Research on Women at Wellesley College, and architect of the S.E.E.D. Project on Inclusive Curriculum (Seeing Educational Equity and Diversity) has made an extraordinary contribution to our understanding of white-skin privilege; her work goes a long way toward answering the question why so many of the privileged "put up with it" so easily. "I think whites are carefully taught not to recognize white privilege, as males are taught not to recognize male privilege. So I have begun in an untutored way to ask what it is like to have white privilege as an invisible package of unearned assets which I can count on cashing in each day, but about which I was 'meant' to remain oblivious."[17] McIntosh's final list has 49 items; she invites us to add to it. I will reproduce below about half of the list so that white-skinned persons of conscience will be motivated to hunt down the rest of her work:

1. I can if I wish arrange to be in the company of people of my race most of the time.

2. If I should need to move, I can be pretty sure of renting or purchasing housing in an area which I can afford and in which I would want to live.

3. I can be pretty sure that my neighbors in such a location will be neutral or pleasant to me.

4. I can go shopping alone most of the time, pretty well assured that I will not be followed or harassed.

5. I can turn on the television or open to the front page of the paper and see people of my race widely represented.

6. When I am told about our national heritage or about "civilization," I am shown that people of my color made it what it is. . . .

9. I can go into . . . a supermarket and find the staple foods which fit with my cultural traditions, into a hairdresser's shop and find someone who can cut my hair.

10. Whether I use checks, credit cards, or cash, I can count on my skin color not to work against the appearance of financial reliability.

11. I can arrange to protect my children most of the time from people who might not like them.

12. I can swear, or dress in second hand clothes or not answer letters, without having people attribute these choices to the bad morals, the poverty, or the illiteracy of my race.

13. I can speak in public to a powerful male group without putting my race on trial. . . .

15. I am never asked to speak for all the people of my racial group.

16. I can remain oblivious of the language and customs of persons of color who constitute the world's majority without feeling in my culture any penalty for such oblivion. . . .

18. I can be pretty sure that if I ask to talk to "the person in charge," I will be facing a person of my race.

19. If a traffic cop pulls me over . . . I can be sure I haven't been singled out because of my race. . . .

22. I can take a job with an affirmative action employer without having co-
workers on the job suspect that I got it because of race.

23. I can choose public accommodation without fearing that people of my race
cannot get in or will be mistreated in the places I have chosen. . . .

25. If my day, week, or year is going badly, I need not ask of each negative episode
or situation whether it has racial overtones. . . .[18]

When I read this for the first time, not so long ago, I was astonished: how
could I have failed to notice so much about being white, I, who had, at least
on one occasion, risked my life in the Civil Rights movement? I was disturbed, too, at my ignorance of what it must be like for people of color to bear
the daily burden of racism. McIntosh says that whites are "carefully taught"
not to notice all this. Paradoxically, we whites have thoroughly learned
something we were not in fact "carefully taught." "Carefully taught" implies
that there were other whites, not so oblivious, who taught us to be oblivious.
But I think that the people who taught me were themselves as oblivious as I
have been myself. Segregation was carefully maintained, as I was growing up
(in the North) in virtually every domain of life. Without black friends or
neighbors, with nary a black teacher from kindergarten through graduate
school, who was there to teach me the difference? I have read all the "important" black writers, but their topic is largely their experience of racism,
not the phenomenology of white skin privilege. McIntosh makes another
quite crucial observation about privilege: some of the items on her list characterized as "privileges," e.g., fair housing, shouldn't be characterized as privileges at all but as entitlements available to all; nor is No. 16, obliviousness
to much of the world's culture, properly a privilege; it is described more accurately as a form of domination as well as a source of intellectual and moral
impoverishment.

Guilt in the Form of a Debt
Nietzsche makes much of the nonmoral origins of moral notions. In *The Genealogy of Morals* he finds the genesis of guilt in a sense of indebtedness; to be
guilty, is to owe someone something. Indeed, the German word *Schuld* has
both meanings, guilt and debt.[19] Here is another gloss on the gulf between
feeling and fact: one can in fact owe someone a debt without knowing it or,
as in the case of the chronic deadbeat, without feeling any urgency, ever, to
repay it.

To owe a debt to someone and to overlook it is blameworthy. What I am
about to say now is very personal; it may be more a personal confession than

a social fact. For many years, Jews and blacks had a special relationship. In comparison with other white Americans, Jews supported black causes financially and politically, far in excess of their representation in the white population. Reasons for this are not hard to find. Both groups had then and still have common enemies (the KKK, the Aryan Nation, etc.). Jews, who had been oppressed for centuries were able more easily than many white Americans to identify with oppressed blacks. Recently, however, these ties have been weakened considerably, chiefly by the rise of black anti-Semitism (how sad that one of the few things blacks are allowed to share with "real Americans" is Jew-hating and Jew-baiting), the identification of many persons of color in this country with the Palestinians, and the emergence of a small but influential group of Jewish neoconservatives who have polemicized against what most blacks see as important to their community's welfare, e.g., affirmative action. But in spite of it all, these ties have not been entirely broken. Jewish financial support is still strong, nor did Jesse Jackson's "Hymietown" remark keep a majority of Jews from voting for him some years ago when he ran in the New York presidential primary.

Whatever the vicissitudes of relations between blacks and Jews, I have always seen blacks in this country as stand-ins for Jews in the following sense: they are standing in a place where we would be if they were not already in it. They have been the first ordered out of the trenches; we Jews are behind the lines, protected in the victim-reserves. There is a place in the mass American psyche (and, so it appears, in the collective psyches of many other peoples as well) for a kind of murderous bigotry. Blacks have mainly occupied this place in this country. In the West, Chinese were in it for a short time; there are parts of this country in which prejudice against Hispanics is very vicious and very widespread. But in the East, the South, and the Midwest, anti-black racism is clearly the principal form of bigotry and the one that has had the most baneful consequences—from the lynching, rape, and mutilation of blacks to de jure and de facto segregation.

But anti-Semitism has been a persistent theme as well. Though he was only one (even one is one too many), Leo Frank, the Jewish manager of a textile plant, in the South, was accused falsely of rape, dragged from his cell, and lynched—largely because he was a Jew. I do not mean by referring to this one incident to put in shadow the regular lynching, castration, and often the burning of black bodies that was common practice in the South but also in the North for decades, ignored by federal law enforcement, often aided and abetted by local police.[20] Children were often brought to these lynchings which sometimes took on the character of a festival. The Ku Klux Klan, reached its peak membership, not in the South, but in the Midwest in the early 1920s. In 1922, for example, one-third of white native-born males in Indiana were members of the Klan. In this incarnation, the Klan was at least as anti-Catholic and anti-Semitic as it was anti-black.[21]

My sense of it is this: they, the blacks, took the heat and the hate and the persecution that might otherwise have been visited upon us, the Jews. Perform a thought-experiment: close your eyes and imagine that overnight, all the blacks and Hispanics disappear: who would be on the front lines then? Of course, no one can know for certain, but even a superficial acquaintance with American history and contemporary politics suggests an answer: gays, lesbians, and, most likely, Jews. We would move up a notch on the register of national scapegoats. Hence, as a Jew, I have often felt indebted to blacks; they have suffered the persecution in some form of which might well have been visited upon us, if the course of U.S. history had been different. Jews in this country have, at least since World War II, not only been little affected by anti-Semitism (one can always think of exceptional cases) but have been allowed to prosper. It is now and has always been payback time: one way to deal with this incalculable debt is to strike a blow, indeed, many blows against antiblack racism.

In Lieu of a Conclusion

I have been arguing, in line with traditional moral psychology, that guilt is a response to the recognition that more privileged Americans, have been complicit in the violation of moral principles. Moreover, guilt is not simply an "emotion" of self-assessment, involving as it does, acts of cognition and certain ideological commitments. In contradistinction to traditional moral psychology, I have argued that guilt is also a moral-existential predicament, i.e., that the reactionary goals pursued by our foreign policy as well as the very structure of everyday life places the relatively privileged in a morally compromised position, whether we know we are in it or not. One can be guilty without feeling guilty and without having authored the social arrangements that involve one in complicity.

So conservatives are quite right to pillory "bleeding hearts"—if bleeding is all they do. The liberal social policies that have been adopted in one or another "war on poverty" may be flawed, but if they are, it is unlikely that their flaws are due to an excess of compassion on the part of policymakers. It is sometimes difficult to believe that conservatives have hearts at all. It is unlikely that the "welfare reform" they support (with the collusion of Democrats) will reduce either poverty or racism to any appreciable degree and it has the potential to impose new forms of suffering and denial on the poor.

There are, of course, extenuating circumstances. Whites grew up in a land that managed to make us oblivious to white skin privilege. I was in my thirties before I began to grasp the enormity as well as the imperceptibility of male privilege under patriarchy; only later was I led to a recognition of the imperceptibility of my own white skin. It is true in law, but is it not true in ethics as well that "ignorance of the law is no excuse"?

I would distinguish between ordinary ignorance and culpable ignorance. I have some extremely sheltered white students from distant suburbs who have grown up, as I did myself, in entirely white communities, educated by school and media to be unaware of the inequality and injustice that deforms our society. Most have never been in downtown Chicago, which has been represented to them as mortally dangerous, have never had a friend of color, and have never come up against a view of U.S. society that is in conflict with what they were taught. When they finally see a ghetto (our university is in the middle of the inner city) or talk to a welfare recipient or meet with an "out" gay person, their confusion and astonishment are palpable. I think that these young people suffer—to use one of their favorite expressions—"cluelessness."

I am less sure of what to say about their parents. Many parents commute: they have some familiarity with the city; they read the papers. How can anyone read the Chicago papers day after day without coming to see that conditions in the ghetto are so terrible that a collective escape from them—without help—would be nothing short of miraculous? Unlike their children who know very little, they know something about "capital flight," rising inequalities in income, our irrational and unfair system of school funding; perhaps they know that 300,000 manufacturing jobs have left the Chicago area in the last 15 years. Their behavior does not manifest simple ignorance: they exhibit culpable ignorance: the willful not-knowing of what is staring them in the face, the bad faith of pretending not to know, what they do indeed know and the retreat under the two-pillared shelter (the disadvantaged are personally responsible; the disadvantaged are biologically unfit) for whites endangered by—the possibility of guilt.[22]

How much effort on the part of a person will cancel her complicity, hence remove her guilt? Can this cancellation ever be complete? In regard to the first form of complicity I discussed, complicity in the crimes of my government, I think that the answer to this question is, in principle, "yes." The people of "Operation Plowshares" (symbolically) attacked missile silos containing nuclear bombs and then, in some cases, were given long jail sentences when they refused to show contrition or promise that there would be no further such actions. These protesters, to my mind, successfully detached themselves from the insanity of Mutually Assured Destruction. But what about antinuclear protesters—protesters of many mad and oppressive policies—who do not devote the better part of their lives to what offends them most, who have not risked their lives or even their jobs, who have not gone to jail? What about the many who "only" wrote letters and sent checks and perhaps attended a few demonstrations?

Again: how much effort on the part of a person will cancel her complicity, hence remove her guilt? I am inclined to the view that in many respects it cannot be canceled; hence my designation of a certain kind of guilt as "existential," my sympathy with Sartre's view (and Plato's) that one cannot have clean hands where the polity is unclean. It is important to remember that there are some inequalities from which we cannot entirely divorce ourselves, no matter how hard we try. White skin privilege is a case in point, as a good part of this privilege consists in experiences that, as a white person, I will never have. I cannot be stopped by the police because I am driving "too good a car" for a person of my color. On the other hand, I can try in my day-to-day living and working to be cognizant of my situation and especially to be cognizant of the situations of my colleagues, students, and friends of color. Julia LeSage, film critic, filmmaker, and activist, once told me that any class which does not mention racism perpetuates it. This seems especially salient to those of us who teach feminist studies, ethics, and political philosophy.

In my view, we accomplish little as individuals; in the spirit of Mother Jones, we need to organize, not to mourn and not merely to "bleed." We need certainly not worry over degrees of complicity—which can become a new and insidious form of white evasion, a back-handed way of keeping ourselves still in the center. We need to find those organizations that appear to be making a difference, join them, and support them. I do not believe that personal change must precede political action, a common New Age belief. Meaningful political action will change us; the relationship between personal change and political empowerment is complex: each needs the other. Neither can be fully successful in the absence of the other. How much time, effort, money, and sacrifice is required for the verdict "no longer complicit"? Or even "no longer as complicit"? This is a question for which there is, I think, no possibility of a blanket answer, for much depends on the kind of injustice that moves us to action, on the state of our health and strength, on our circumstances and responsibilities to those close to us, and, to some extent, on the political climate of the country. My conclusion then, is that this discussion has raised questions about the shedding of guilt and the termination of complicity for which there are no conclusive answers.

Notes

I would like to thank Professor Claudia Card for her inestimable help in the preparation of this chapter. But I alone am responsible for the ideas expressed herein; she bears no responsibility for my limitations. I would also like to thank Ted Precht for his invaluable assistance as well.

This chapter was previously published in *On Feminist Ethics and Politics*, edited by Claudia Card (Lawrence: University Press of Kansas, 1999).

1. Bill Gates, CEO of Microsoft, is, at the time of this writing (1998), said to be the richest man in the United States.

2. George Gilder, *Wealth and Poverty* (New York: Bantam Books, 1982).

3. None of what I say here should be construed as a defense of liberalism as a political theory.

4. See Gabriele Taylor, *Pride, Shame and Guilt: Emotions of Self-Assessment* (Oxford: Oxford University Press, 1985).

5. The sort of complicity I have in mind is "moral" complicity, but perhaps "legal" complicity is not far off the mark if we think not primarily of U.S. law but of international law. *Black's Law Dictionary* defines "complicity" as "participation in guilt."

6. Franz Kafka, *The Trial* (New York: Alfred A. Knopf, 1959), 7.

7. The suburban specialists told me unequivocally that I should quit graduate school and get married. It was not until I found a doctor on my own, Bertram Carnow, that I was taken seriously. Carnow told me that the graduate students he saw in his Hyde Park practice (from the University of Chicago) suffered more from stress related illnesses than soldiers he had seen as a front-line surgeon in World War II.

8. Alison Jaggar, *Feminist Politics and Human Nature* (Totowa, N.J.: Rowman & Allanheld, 1983), esp. chap. 3.

9. Richard J. Herrnstein and Charles Murray, *The Bell Curve* (New York: Free Press, 1994).

10. But see, e.g., Ruth Bleier, *Science and Gender: A Critique of "Biology and Its Theories about Women"* (New York: Pergamon Press, 1989).

11. Herrnstein and Murray, *The Bell Curve*. (Gould's extremely persuasive critique of research of this sort is based in part on a very telling attack on the scientificity of I.Q. tests, Herrnstein and Murray's principal research instrument. See Stephen Jay Gould, *The Mismeasure of Man* (New York: Norton, 1981).

12. There is some debate currently about the biological bases of homosexuality. Many lesbians, however, claim to have made a choice, for many feminists, a principled political choice. The "reasons" offered by homophobes for denying gays and lesbians not just privileges, but basic rights are either empirically false (homosexuals are always recruiting the naive into the homosexual lifestyle) or they are based on readings of the Bible that (a) have been challenged by many scholars of religion and (b) have no place in a secular society anyhow. See John Boswell, *Christianity and Social Tolerance* (Chicago: University of Chicago Press, 1978).

13. Jean-Paul Sartre, "Dirty Hands," in *No Exit and Three Other Plays* (New York: Vintage, 1955), 170–71.

14. Ibid., 171.

15. However, many people tithe; there is sharing in times of emergency, even extraordinary acts of courage in times of emergency. We are egotists, but also, under certain conditions, altruists.

16. See Sandra Bartky, "Sympathy and Solidarity," in this volume (chapter 4).

17. Peggy McIntosh, "White Privilege: Unpacking the Invisible Knapsack," *Peace and Freedom* (July–August 1989), 10. See also McIntosh, "White Privilege and Male Privilege: A Personal Account of Coming to See Correspondences through Work in Women's Studies," Working Paper No. 189, 1988, Wellesley College Center for Research on Women.

18. Ibid., 44.

19. Friedrich Nietzsche, *The Genealogy of Morals*, trans. Horace B. Samuel (London: T. N. Foulis, Ltd., 1922), 79 and *passim*. Nietzsche's discussion of this connection is rich in both psychoanalytic and theological insights.

20. Seventy blacks were lynched in 1919 alone, fourteen were burned. M. William Lutholtz, *Grand Dragon: D.C. Stephenson and the Ku Klux Klan in Indiana* (West Lafayette, Ind.: Purdue University Press, 1991), 154.

21. Ibid., 55.

22. On this form of bad faith, see in particular Lewis Gordon, *Bad Faith and Antiblack Racism* (Atlantic Highlands, N.J.: Humanities Press, 1995).

~

CHAPTER EIGHT

Race, Complicity,
and Culpable Ignorance

We cannot wait for the undamaged to make our connections for us; we can't
wait to speak until we are wholly clear and righteous. There is no purity in
our lifetimes, no end to the process.

—Adrienne Rich (Split at the Root)[1]

I

Racism, like sexism, is a complex phenomenon having historical, psychoanalytic, political, social, and economic roots; it is, to my mind, still not completely understood. I wish to examine what does (or does not) go on in the
minds of "nice" white people which allows them to ignore the terrible effects
of racism and, to the extent that these effects are recognized at all, to deny
that they bear any responsibility for their perpetuation.[2]

When I was just sixteen, I left my comfortable suburb to attend a large
state university several hundred miles away. By my sophomore year I had developed an idea of the university which, because it fulfilled my own needs
and fantasies so well, I did not discard until much later. The university, as I
saw it, was an island of sanity in a mad and malevolent world, a refuge from
the money-grubbing, vulgarity, and bigotry that surrounded it. Of course
there were racist incidents and racist individuals on the campus but I saw
them as *exceptions* that didn't really belong there. The university, after all,
was a gathering place for educated people and such people I understood to
have long abandoned, if they ever had them, racist notions, any kind of

racism being, of course intellectually primitive. The exceptions I saw every-where (but in a mode of denial) were somehow not of the *essence* of the place. I assumed that persons of color would view the university within the same essence and accidents schema I had adopted myself.

It took me an inordinate amount of time and much reeducation to face up to the manifestly racist climate of most higher education. Located in a city which is about half black, except for the important African-American Stud-ies Program, the university that employs me largely ignores the culture and history of African-Americans. There are few African-American professors.³ Students can graduate and so be regarded officially as "educated persons" without once having to confront in any formal way the pervasive racism, not to mention the sexism and class oppression of American society. The "mul-ticulturalism" requirement can be satisfied by taking courses, none of which confront the realities of race, class, or gender *today*. As we are largely a com-muter campus, we have been spared the widespread racial hatred that cur-rently disfigures many residential campuses, though the few dormitories we have erected are beset from time to time by ugly racial incidents. The wash-rooms are full of racist graffiti. I taught in a large classroom once in which someone had carefully carved on a door directly at my eye level "Kill Nig-gers." Apart from official groups such as the Concert Band and Student Gov-ernment, as far as I know, there are no effectively integrated social groups on our campus, a departure from possibilities of mixing that still prevailed dur-ing my undergraduate days. The segregation on campus seems to have been mutually agreed upon by both blacks and whites. Chicago, after all, is home to notorious residential segregation as well as the Nation of Islam, a leading proponent of black separatism.

The relentlessly white and middle-class cultural style of the university as an institution in effect marginalizes the speech and cultural style of non-white students. The failure of whites to see the official style *as* a style, i.e., as thoroughly particular and not just "the way things are," is another manifes-tation of what Bulhan calls "the shameful livery of white incomprehension."⁴ In spite of substantial diversity among the students (only 46 percent are Cau-casian), the whiteness of the official campus culture must bear heavily on many students of color. The term "culture shock" sounds very banal and plat-itudinous unless you yourself have experienced it. I have, once, so I report on the suffering it caused me. I was invited to be a visiting professor at an Ivy League school. I was a Midwesterner, a state university product through and through, a Jew whose grandmothers were both illiterate. I had never been anywhere near the Ivy League; moreover, this particular school had begun to admit women only ten years earlier. During my first three weeks I lived in a kind of disguised panic. Everyone was very kind. But the feeling that I didn't belong in that pristine town, in those paneled rooms, sitting in wing chairs beneath oil paintings of elite WASP worthies haunted me. I was haunted too by the fear that my colleagues and students would see immediately that I was incompetent, a fraud and an interloper. Living alone, I often woke up in the middle of the night in a cold sweat, fists clenched, my body in a fetal position. My fear was so great that I ceased menstruating. Now none of this lasted very long and things turned out well for me but it lasted long enough to disabuse me of the notion that "culture shock" is a meaningless cliché. How much worse it must be for many of our students of color than it was for me at this elite college, a white person after all, with a Ph.D. and publications. How much worse it must be for students coming for the first time out of lives lived almost entirely in a segregated world. We know that many people feel the university to be an alien place, a place in which they "don't belong."[5] But I fear that there are modes of suffering attached to this feeling of "not belonging" that many in the dominant culture have not yet fathomed.

How shocked I was when I discovered, late in my career, that I was regarded by many students of color as a racist. I thought that I was sending them coded messages to the contrary—by my manner and by the frequency with which I mentioned racism and assigned readings on the topic of racism in courses in ethics and social and political philosophy.

Alas, such was not the case. I imagine that they were not attuned to subtleties in the classroom because their whole experience of the white world had been one of stigma at best or of gross racism at worst. When Harold Washington became the first black mayor of Chicago, he won with a solid black vote and with 10 percent of the white vote. Given the racial realities of Chicago, it was certainly reasonable for my students to assume that I was in the 90 percent who voted against him. It disturbed me that they might assume that I approved of the gang members—or police—who would beat them up if they crossed one of the shifting but invisible boundaries that define where your turf is in Chicago—and where it's worth your life to wander onto alien turf. They believed, I think, that I was the kind of person who wouldn't live next door to a black family or have a black friend. Because I was a racist, everything I said or did was suspect. The bad grades I gave them on poorly written papers (with copious suggestions for improvement and invitations to tutor) were seen as just another way of keeping them from getting better jobs and a better life. Everything I said was misheard because it came out of a white mouth. When I said that persons of color were often given the dirtiest and most poorly paid jobs in our society, they bristled. They took this as an insult to their parents who often had such jobs; they reminded me of the dignity of all honest labor. It seemed incredible to me that anyone as interested as I was in examining theories of racism and in probing the relationship of racism and sexism could still be seen as a visceral racist, but there it was. Thinking about this later, I assume that they assumed that playing with ideas was a kind of game for me, a game that had little to do with real life. It became clear to me how corrosive segregation had been for all of us: the basic trust that students need to have in their teachers was lacking. Indeed, why shouldn't it be lacking? I was white.

Now these attitudes varied somewhat with the class position of my students of color. The poorer students had never encountered whites except as oppressors. Middle-class African-Americans were far less hostile, less resistant; perhaps they had encountered less police harassment, were entirely independent of an oppressive white welfare establishment; perhaps their high schools were integrated. Things are easier for me now, but only because the graduates of inner-city high schools have, for a variety of reasons, now largely disappeared from this inner-city university. I am able to speak to students about racism more honestly and openly now, having allowed myself to see their version of the university and having disburdened myself of a fantasized university that existed only in my imagination.

II

I argued in "In Defense of Guilt" (chapter 7) that most white people in this country are complicit in an unjust system of race relations that bestows unearned advantages on them while denying these advantages to racial Others. Complicity in this system is neither chosen nor, typically, is it acknowledged, because there are both powerful ideological systems in place that serve to reassure whites that the suffering of darker-skinned Others is not of their doing and because the capacity of whites to live in denial of responsibility is very highly developed. Another powerful factor has to do with the invisibility of white-skin privilege to white people, consisting as it does in *what does not typically happen to them*—like racial profiling (more about this later).

What follows is a classification of phenomenologies of denial on the part of "nice" white people, people who believe that they have no race prejudice and get very upset and often quite angry when told that they bear some responsibility for the persistence of such prejudice. By "nice people" I mean people who are appalled at incidents of violence directed to persons of color (but not nice enough to do very much about them) and who thoroughly disapprove of fascist skinheads, the Aryan Nation, and the Ku Klux Klan.[6]

There are eight categories altogether. While I have no way of knowing what percentage of "nice" racists belong in what category, there is the suggestion of an answer in the length of my treatment of (5) the culpably ignorant and (6) the self-deceivers.

1. The Fantasists

For the fantasist, the world is not seen as it is but as the fantasist would like it to be. My former idea of the university and my inaccurate idea of how I was perceived by many students, is an excellent case in point. Fantasy takes the place of the often difficult task of first finding out what is really going on and then doing something about it. There are many kinds of fantasy. The most removed from social reality is the flat out denial that there is such a thing as white racism. Racism is seen as an unfortunate aspect of the past that has been superseded. The fact that people still seem exercised about it is explained in a variety of ways, e.g., by continuing demands for such policies as affirmative action which is now no longer needed. The complainers have a chip on their shoulder or else they haven't really made an effort to take advantage of what reforms have been made since the 1960s.

> [W]e are told from many quarters that "race" does not matter, should not matter and so should not be spoken as reference to something which cannot refer to anything at all. We are informed that our country has transcended racism and even color consciousness, that certain Black heroes, from athletes to politicians, have "transcended race" which means only that these individuals are somehow acceptable to white America.[7]

Complaining blacks (and this would include all major black organizations, such as the NAACP) have not taken advantage of policies put in place by well-meaning if somewhat wrong-headed white liberals and so blame everything that is amiss in their lives not on their own lack of effort and ambition, but on whites. I run across people all the time who take racism to be nothing but some kind of excuse of individual or collective on the part of persons of color; this racist strategy has a familiar name: blaming the victim. All sorts of whites fall into this category but I associate it principally with conservative politicians and some businesspersons. The latter point out the irrationality of racism: it is in the interest of business to hire the most qualified, so discrimination on the basis of race or gender is potentially counterproductive, i.e., it artificially limits the hiring pool. Because race prejudice is irrational and business is rational, racism cannot exist, at least in this domain.

2. The "Tu-quoque" (you too) Racists

These whites do not deny that there is such a thing as white racism (though they themselves are of course free of it) but there is black racism, too. Louis Farrakhan has done much to feed the perception among whites that there is widespread black racism, taking the form in his movement principally of anti-Semitism. His followers, for example, were told that Jewish doctors infected black children with AIDS. His predecessor in the Nation of Islam, Elijah Muhammad, consistently referred to whites as "devils," which in his scheme of things was not meant metaphorically but literally. The "tu quoque" whites appear to have developed the following rationalization: black and white racism more or less balance each other out, this in the following ways: no matter what we whites might do for blacks and we have done much (arguably), they will hate us anyhow, hence poisoning progressive social policies. Whatever we do, hatred and bigotry will not be overcome, they will simply be recapitulated, now with different victims—us. We have acted already, so let them get their house in order. While there is certainly black racism, the "tu quoques" entirely ignore the vast discrepancies in scope and in particular, the effect on peoples' lives of the two racisms. This avoidance strategy in effect reifies hatred and bigotry; they become facts of nature, like the weather, removed from human agency, hence human responsibility.

3. The Clueless

Fantasists see racism as, in principle, already overcome; the tu quoques minimize it. The clueless have no effective understanding of racism at all. No one belongs in this category who has grown up in a large city or is over eighteen years old. But there are many white young people who have grown up in places far distant from the inner city who are fearful of going there: too dangerous, they have been told, or too bewildering, too many people utterly unlike the people they know. Since Polish (largely undocumented) women are replacing blacks as cleaners in the tonier suburbs of Chicago, since few if any blacks live in these places and since racism and other controversial topics are ignored in most high schools, it is likely that these students or other young people in such situations are indeed clueless. They appear never to watch the dwindling number of TV documentaries that reveal the less attractive features of American life (like PBS *Frontline*); instead, they watch sitcoms and MTV. They appear not to read the newspapers or to take very seriously anything that happened before they were born. Without information or exposure, many have absorbed the sort of racism that is pervasive in white society, a racism of stereotypes and "common sense" ("there are plenty of jobs for those who want to work"). They mouth the usual racist banalities with no understanding that they themselves are racist—a label they vehemently reject.

4. The Deplorers

There are those who recognize racism for the evil it is. They deplore it. They are full of sympathy for the plight of the stigmatized and despised, but make at best a few futile attempts to do something about it; often they do nothing about it. Deploring becomes a substitute for action as well as a salve for the conscience. Unwilling to make themselves unpopular with their families or in their own social circles, they never challenge publicly the use of racist language, the telling of racist jokes, or the frequent reassurances whites give each other that they are innocent of antiblack racism. Antiracist whites should try (unless certain conditions make this impossible) not to listen to racist language, racist jokes, or racist misinformation, wherever and whenever they hear it.

I do not think that we will change very many minds in this way, but people who express racist sentiments need to know that they cannot confidently expect to do this just anywhere, that they cannot count on affirmation from people in their own social circles. They need to know that there might well be a price to be paid for this kind of talk even if the currency is only embarrassment.

5. The Culpably Ignorant

"Culpable ignorance" I define as the failure to know what one ought to know, when such a failure implicates one in a moral lapse. For example, thousands of white people commute into the racially mixed inner city from outlying, largely lily-white suburbs. These commuters pass through the blighted neighborhoods of the poor twice a day. Most read the newspapers (indeed, what is a commuter without his newspaper?). The newspapers are full of shocking stories about the dreadful conditions that prevail in thousands of public housing units in the inner city. Much can be gleaned from just looking out the windows of the commuter trains. Thus, these white people are not simply ignorant in the way the clueless are ignorant. They are in a position to know; sometimes they need only to open their eyes to the living conditions of the poor and poorer (i.e., the homeless). Such people have chosen to be ignorant, culpably ignorant. These are fairly sophisticated people; they must know something about our unfair system of public school financing that gives their own children a vastly better education than is given to black children in the projects. Since they must read the business news too, they know of capital flight and the ensuing large loss of industrial jobs in the rust belts of

Chicago's South Side, Gary, and other northern cities. Indeed, three hundred thousand industrial jobs have been lost in Chicago in the last fifteen years. Whom do they think held these jobs? What do they think may have happened to the people who held these jobs? What provisions were made to secure alternate employment for workers whose jobs fled to cheaper and more reliable, because more repressive, labor venues? What happens to the poor when public housing in their soon-to-be-trendy neighborhoods is torn down? They—the culpably ignorant—do not know.

An extreme limiting case of culpable ignorance was reported recently in the *Wall Street Journal* (April 2, 2001). An African-American lineman, Cornelius Cooper, and two others have brought suit against Georgia Power Co. and its parent, Southern Power Co. Cooper, a twenty-five-year employee alleges that he was passed over for promotions, that black employees were routinely given lower pay than white employees for the same jobs, and that, as a black, he was subjected to racial slurs and repeatedly spray-painted in his genital area by white employees. Worse, co-workers made light of lynchings, tied hangman's nooses in his presence, and often left such knots displayed in company facilities. Attached to the charges, was an 8-by-10 color photograph of a noose hanging inside a company building in Cornelia, Georgia. The article continues: "Executives at Georgia Power and its parent company were taken aback. But their surprise wasn't at finding a noose on the premises; it was in discovering that African-Americans could be offended by one." Former Southern Chairman and Chief Executive Officer A. W. "Bill" Dahlberg said in a deposition "I had no earthly idea that anybody today would consider that to be a racial symbol. None whatsoever."

An internal investigation by the company turned up a total of thirteen ropes tied as nooses in eight Georgia Power facilities. The executives said that one hangman's noose, wrapped around the neck of a skeleton, was an ex-smoker's personal reminder to stop smoking. The plaintiffs later filed a photograph taken recently of an additional noose tied around the neck of a crudely made black figure and allegedly left at the desk of a black employee. These and other incidents of racial harassment were reported to management, which did nothing to stop them. The current CEO of Georgia Power, David M. Ratcliffe, says that he too didn't think of nooses "in a racial context" until the filing of the lawsuit, nor did many other white managers at the company. Ratcliffe maintains that "the failure to realize that black workers might be sensitive to nooses doesn't indicate that management was indifferent to the issue of racial hostility in the workplace."

One scarcely knows what to think about this amazing tale; indeed, one doesn't know whether to laugh or cry. Is this really just a case of extreme culpable ignorance or is it old-fashioned hard-core racism? In order to know for sure, one would have to be able to get into the heads of these white managers. I have classified this as the *ne plus ultra* of culpable ignorance for two reasons: first, "Bill" Dahlberg's willingness to portray himself in the media as an idiot; surely a hard-core racist would have found something less embarrassing and more self-protective to say. Second, hard-core racists who understood the meaning of these nooses would certainly have seen a lawsuit in the offing and taken steps to stop the harassment. That they did not lends some small measure of credibility to their defense, to what their attorneys will have no choice but to construe as culpable ignorance.

6. The Self Deceivers

These "nice" and not so nice whites know a great deal about racism. They are culpable but not ignorant. Their strategy is to deny that they bear any responsibility either for maintaining or for perpetuating the racial caste hierarchy. They deny what they do in fact know; they know what they know, as Sartre would say, in the mode of not knowing it. They are in what Sartre, Beauvoir, and Lewis Gordon call "bad faith."[8] The guilt of the privileged—and complicity is a form of guilt—is not attached to any particular act or policy; guilt of this sort is occasioned by something far more global, namely, the very structure of the social totality itself that positions some as privileged, others as underprivileged. These positions are determined largely but not always irrevocably by the accidents of birth.

The complicity to which I refer is not legal complicity but moral complicity: am I stretching the idea of complicity too far? I think not. Complicity, like all guilt, follows upon the violation of a law or principle to which the agent has given his or her allegiance. While there need be no violation of law in the juridical sense, the racist system clearly violates a moral principle. One way of expressing the principle is this: "It is wrong to enjoy privileges from which other people have been unjustly excluded, especially if one's privileges have been predicated upon the unjust exclusion of others." White skin privilege, says Peggy McIntosh, is "an invisible package of unearned assets which I can count on cashing in each day" but about which I am oblivious.[9] McIntosh lists forty-nine unearned privileges. I will reproduce three of them in order to give the flavor of her work: (1) Whether I use checks, credit cards, or cash. I can count on my skin color not to work against the appearance of financial reliability; (2) I can arrange to protect my children most of the time from people who might not like them; (3) When I am told about our national heritage or about "civilization," I am shown that people of my color made it what it is. Jane Lazarre, in her superb *Beyond the Whiteness of Whiteness*, offers her own testimony:

> I think of all the times I felt white, powerfully white, obliviously white, visibly white, shamefully white: seeing a policeman come toward me at night and feeling the relief of this protection, walking into a country store in a strange town with no sense of anxiety that I might frighten the owner . . . feeling myself at the center when scholars talk about "women's history" and "women's rights"; planning my life, all of my life, constructing my dreams, without taking race into consideration at all. (41)[10]

White skin privilege is importantly an absence; it consists in what does not happen to *me*. Marxists are right to point to the systematically deceptive character of everyday reality; the peculiar nature of white skin privilege feeds the bad faith of "nice" racists.

Are whites then off the hook of complicity because they are often oblivious to their privilege? I think that the answer to this is "no." White skin privilege is merely one of the many ingredients that go to make up white racism. Michael Stocker has rejected the conventional view that more and better education will eliminate or at least lessen bigotry. Stocker maintains that it is often quite false that knowledge of the Other will produce sympathy for the Other, much less liking for her.[11] While I think that we have no choice except to pursue more and better education of ourselves and others around issues of racism, I think Stocker's point is this: many white people think that they already have knowledge of the Other and that what they know absolves them of any complicity with racism. But what they know is false, sometimes mythic (the black welfare queen) or it is a mixture of fabrication and ideology. I define "ideology" as a set of beliefs that bears some resemblance to social reality, but not enough to qualify as "knowledge." The principal effect of ideology is to mystify social reality: if some system of ideas were flatly and obviously false, it would be less effective as mystification.

There are (at least) four sets of ideological beliefs that justify the deprived and subordinate position of poor blacks: (1) their alleged character defects; (2) their "culture of poverty"; (3) the skewed policies of welfare liberals; and (4) their biological inferiority. In regard to (1), many white people believe that blacks are lazy and promiscuous; hence, they deserve their fate. But even if this were true, would their children deserve *their* fate? The question is never posed. Rates of illegitimacy are about equal between white and black society; everything depends on the resources of the family into which the child is born, not whether it is born inside or outside of wedlock. The hypocrisy in regard to this issue is simply staggering. Over a million young black men who have virtually no other way to make a decent living than to "deal" are currently in prison; then, these same young men are raked over the coals for not being upstanding bourgeois husbands and fathers.

Louis Althusser has claimed that ideology is not always flatly false, but reflects a deceptive and superficial aspect of the social totality.[12] Now there is certainly a relationship between exertion and reward; everyone knows this. So the sight of young men in ghetto neighborhoods lounging about the streets when others are at work *seems* to justify the claim that blacks are not really trying. There are of course complex determinants for this sight other than "laziness": to name a few, capital flight and the disappearance of jobs that earlier in this century blacks were recruited from the South to do; the lack of available capital for entrepreneurship; the long history of denial of credit to blacks that made entrepreneurship virtually impossible;[13] a failing public school system; lack of investment in ghetto neighborhoods; the avoidance by many middle-class blacks of those unfortunates who have been left behind; the persistence of race prejudice; etc. etc. It takes some effort to get the whole story, some kind of goodwill toward the unfortunate to try to see how the world looks from their point of view. Where this measure of goodwill is lacking, those men lounging on the corner tell the white spectator everything he wants to know. ("There are plenty of jobs for those who want to work.") Jobs available to the inner-city poor, as is or should be well known, are minimum wage jobs that do not raise a family above the poverty line.

There has also been an effort to show that black family structure is responsible for poverty and violence in the ghetto (Moynihan). The story is supposed to go like this: black families are matriarchal. The boys in these families have no decent male role models and so, to separate psychologically from the mother (and many mothers are quite harsh, hoping this will save their sons from the street), the boys rebel against the mother and her values and adopt an exaggerated version, indeed, a fantasized version of masculinity that issues in violence and antisocial behavior. Many blacks themselves believe that strong fathers would produce well-behaved sons. (Hence the Million Man March.) The youth gang is supposed to be one consequence of "black matriarchy." But youth gangs are a result of poverty. There were violent Jewish, Irish, and Italian gangs in Chicago earlier in the last century when their communities were poor and they themselves were often despised. These gang members came largely from intact families with strong fathers.

Conservatives like George Gilder (*Wealth and Poverty*) have argued that well-meaning liberals have essentially corrupted the black poor by keeping them on the dole so long that they lost all incentive to "pull themselves up by their bootstraps." So liberals are often flogged these days with having *created* black poverty, not with failing to develop policies that would have eliminated it. One of the problems with this line of thinking is that welfare payments were never large enough to allow those who received them to do much more than merely subsist. Compare this to a massive program of largely white welfare, the GI Bill. Millions of veterans were helped to support themselves and their families while their trade school or college tuition was paid. This allowed a large number of (white) men to raise themselves from working-class status into the middle class, with concomitant improvements in salaries and living conditions. Some government programs have demonstrably helped persons who suffer from discrimination: to mention two, Headstart and affirmative action. Indeed, the latter is credited with having helped to create a substantial black middle class.

Finally, we come to the hoariest and most ancient theory of black unworthiness, the theory that will not die: blacks are genetically inferior to whites, hence their situation is not our *fault*; it lies in the nature of human biology. Scholarly tomes alleging black biological inferiority, usually in regard to intelligence (*The Bell Curve*) continue to appear like the zombies in *Night of the Living Dead*. Will these creatures never find peace in their graves? Such theories have been rejected overwhelmingly by the most prominent members of the scientific community; nevertheless, "respectable" shapers of public opinion, such as the *New York Times*, while never exactly endorsing these texts, treat them with great respect. Again, there is some mystified "evidence" for endorsing this message: black students in inner-city high schools do less well on standardized tests than white students in affluent suburbs; their drop-out rate is higher, etc. Once more, without the goodwill necessary to look for the causes of poor school performance and high drop-out rates, it is easy to conclude that blacks are unwilling or incapable of the intellectual achievement necessary to overcome endemic poverty. I take it that this absence of goodwill is not a cause but an effect of racism. A modicum of goodwill might well motivate a longer and more critical look at American society. this could change the worldview of "nice" racists, threatening the mental economy that absolves them of any complicity in the established order of domination.

7. The Selfish and Self-Interested

White skin privilege and ideological mystification together do not explain the unwillingness of so many whites to acknowledge complicity. Of course, self-interest plays an important role in all of this. What would it cost to do away with poverty in this country? What would it cost *me*? What if taking all this seriously means that I have to change my life? Would I have to change my life dramatically? Will I have, perhaps, to make some sacrifices? What if I am forcefully reminded of my early religious training? Am I my brother's keeper? If the answer is "yes," what does this "yes" require of me? It seems clear that the answer given by most people in this church-ridden Judeo-Christian land is "no." Given the wealth of our nation, I do not think that very dramatic sacrifices would be demanded of comfortably off persons, but our media, our political establishment, and most of our religious and educational establishments never bring it up. Perhaps we would merely need to divert our tax money away from such projects as Star Wars (which will end up costing not billions, but trillions), the School of the Americas, the escalating number of prisons and costs of keeping so many locked up for victimless crimes, the Columbian military.

8. The Fearful
Psychological factors as well as ideological factors may well be involved in "not knowing what one knows," for example, fear. Crime should not go unpunished. Perhaps we fear retaliation at the hands of those we have wronged or, more accurately, those whose wrongs we have done nothing to right. I have felt this fear myself.

When we do turn our attention to actually doing something about racism, when we begin to commiserate with its victims or take steps to replace our culpable ignorance with knowledge, a whole new host of issues presents itself. Some of us fall under the illusion that heroic acts of identification or of empathic understanding by themselves will relieve us of our oppressors' guilt. Another risk: when one opens oneself fully to the misery of others, we fear being swallowed up in this misery. Now while there are points of similarity between a feeling and that feeling commiserated-with, nonetheless, the two are not identical. I commiserate with your sufferings and take joy in your joys but I experience neither your suffering nor your joy; they are *yours*. Max Scheler is very instructive on this point: "My commiseration and *his* suffering are phenomenologically *two different facts*, not *one* fact . . . a person who has never felt mortal terror can still understand and envisage it" (see chapter 4 above). It seems that we need to walk a tightrope between a life so privatized that our sympathies reach no farther than ourselves, our families, and the occasional lost dog and an empathic identification that dissolves our ego-boundaries and tosses us into a frightening emotional abyss so vast that it would paralyze our ability to act.

There appears to be some kind of space in the minds of many set aside for bigotry, a bigotry that does not fit easily into any of my eight categories of "nice" racists. I have heard whites in rural Michigan who have hardly ever seen a black much less known one personally rail against the ways in which blacks—all imagined to be on welfare—are gnawing away at the nation's substance. Since the passage of "welfare reform"—"hillbillies"—southern Appalachians who have been drifting into Michigan for half a century in search of a better life—have been put into the collective doghouse. What strikes one forcibly is the need for *someone* to be in the doghouse. I am surprised to read that there is still anti-Semitism in Poland, often quite virulent. This is surprising, since the overwhelming majority of Polish Jews were murdered in World War II; it seems that there can be anti-Semitism without Jews.

Another example: My partner is the child of Lithuanian displaced persons. When Lithuanians come to Chicago for good or to visit, one is astonished, within days of their landing to hear issuing forth from many of their mouths, in barely comprehensible English, all the usual racist slanders and canards about black Americans. These people may not know how to buy a stamp or get downtown, but they know that African-Americans are lazy and promiscuous. That place in the mind or brain (depending on your metaphysics) formerly occupied by the Jews or the Poles (Lithuanians hate Poles) is soon filled by antiblack racism. But my partner's mother, whom I have known well for twenty-five years, comes from exactly the same cultural background as most of the newer arrivals, and is entirely free of anti-Semitism, religious, and racial bigotry. But why?

Psychoanalytically oriented writers on racism have put forward the claim that the bigot has projected his own unconscious fears and tabooed desires onto the despised Other; in despising the Other, he is despising "abjected" dimensions of his own person. This theory would explain why the racist so often associates impurity of one sort or another with the racial Other. If we agree, for the sake of argument, that everyone has tabooed erotic and aggressive desires, how do we explain those white foes of racism who *also* had highly sexually repressive upbringings, had too rigorous toilet training, and were taught that the products of their bodies were disgusting?[14] There are persons from similar cultural backgrounds, who have been subjected as children to similar taboos, who do not find it necessary to create a scapegoat for desires they experience, unconsciously, as alien and shameful.

III

I have tried in this chapter to identify some modes of white antiblack racist consciousness, in particular, the kind of consciousness that grasps its own complicity on some level but denies it on another. I do not claim that my catalogue is complete; I call on others to expand it and to refine it.

I argued in the last paragraph of "In Defense of Guilt" (chapter 7) that we can accomplish little as individuals, that complex historical, sociological, and political factors beyond our control rule out the hope that whites can ever have entirely clean hands. I said too that we need to organize to oppose racism, that too much hand-wringing and soul-searching about our own complicity can become still another way of putting whites in the center and relegating blacks to the margins. I cited film critic and feminist theorist Julia Lesage who told me once that every class that does not mention racism perpetuates it (a piece of advice meant primarily for those of us who teach women's studies, ethics, and political theory). I rejected a very common view about social and personal change, i.e., that personal change must come first. I argued that political action and personal transformation condition one another equally. I still believe all of these things, but ruminating on the "phenomenologies" sketched here, I believe that more needs to be said about the state of mind of the "ordinary" racist. We need to know, as I have said, why people from similar social backgrounds turn out so differently: coming from a virulently anti-Semitic culture, my companion's mother, so like her compatriots in every other way, was quite free of this form of bigotry. We need to figure out how white society, or at least more of white society, can get beneath the appearance of things (garbage on ghetto streets; loungers on ghetto street corners; users and dealers in crack and heroin) to the often complex economic and political factors that produce these phenomena—and our role in their perpetuation. "[U]nderstanding racism does not occur automatically or quickly, through an act of will or as a result of simple decency and hatred of prejudice."[15]

I doubt that anything short of a new civil rights movement could begin to do this, and it would have to fight hard for the kind of media coverage that could get the message out to masses of people. Balanced coverage of virtually anything is difficult to impossible in view of the consolidation and corporatization of the mass media. The evil of segregation was comparatively easy to point to: but if the will were there, capital flight, the decline in the manufacturing sector, poor schools, the lack of affordable housing, the racist character of the criminal justice system, etc. could be dramatized without much difficulty. Since most Americans have far more viewing choice than they did in the days of Edward R. Murrow, few people will voluntarily watch documentaries if something more "entertaining" were in competition. Disturbing material would jeopardize profits. That is why the exposé of the conditions that produce poverty and suffering in the lives of disadvantaged persons has to be part of a mass-based movement that is making *news*, that is racially integrated and that takes, as did the last Civil Rights movement, the moral high ground. How else might a sense of public outrage be produced that could begin to function as a counterweight to the pervasive racism that passes in many white venues as "common sense"?[16] Much too should be said about the plight of children, for even if their parents have "bad characters," children must be rescued. This is not to suggest that children should be taken away from their parents, as was done so cruelly with native American children during many decades of the last century. To help children is to help whole families—with job training, daycare, decent housing, drug rehabilitation programs, etc. I share Martin Luther King Jr.'s dream of a "poor peoples' movement," for if programs such as these are not offered to whites in or at the poverty line as well, none of this would be feasible. Indeed, money to finance a successful war on poverty would have to come from people in the higher brackets and from the corporations, many of which pay no tax at all on income. (Is this the "Return of the Fantasist"?)

It is important to show commonalities between whites and blacks: bad faith whites seem to think that the future of their own children is crucial to their commitment as parents but assume too often that black parents don't care. The differences must be revealed too, but this will require tact and delicacy. I believe that many poor people are demoralized and that this demoralization severely limits their sense of agency. But what exactly is demoralization? What are its effects? How can it be combated?

A new civil rights movement would effect massive public education, as did the movement of the 1950s and 1960s. Indeed, we must behave always as if education, more and better education, will prevail, and especially the kind of education that happens not in "Brotherhood Week" but in the course of mass-based political agitation. And white people need to keep in mind what Socrates taught so long ago, at the very dawn of philosophy: Know Thyself! Of course the struggle will always be between David and Goliath, but we should not forget that against all odds, it was David who won.

Notes

1. Adrienne Rich, "Split at the Root," in *Blood, Bread and Poetry, Selected Prose, 1979–1985* (New York: W. W. Norton, 1986), 42. Cited in Jane Lazarre, *Beyond the Whiteness of Whiteness* (Durham and London: Duke University Press, 1996), xvi.

2. The specific sort of racism I shall deal with in the chapter is antiblack racism, especially the racism that targets the black "underclass." I am aware that other minorities suffer discrimination as well.

3. The situation may be changing for the better. I believe that many academic units are making bona fide efforts to hire persons of color. At this moment in time, the College

of Liberal Arts and Sciences is very supportive of the African-American Studies Program, the Latin American Studies Program, and the Gender and Women's Studies Program.

4. Hussein Abdilahi Bulhan, *Frantz Fanon and the Psychology of Oppression* (New York: Plenum Press, 1985).

5. The few white colleagues I have known with working-class origins have told me that they still find the university an alien environment.

6. I write, as is evident, as a white person, of course as a white woman. I myself have not escaped shorter or longer periods of immersion in some of the states of consciousness I shall describe.

7. Lazarre, *Beyond the Whiteness of Whiteness*, 14.

8. Gordon, op. cit.

9. Peggy McIntosh, "White Privilege and Male Privilege: A Personal Account of Coming to See Correspondences through Work in Women's Studies," Working Paper No. 189 (Wellesley, Mass.: Wellesley College Center for Research on Women, 1988), 44.

10. Lazarre, *Beyond the Whiteness of Whiteness*, 41. This beautifully written book is the best account I know of that treats what it is for a white person to really face up to racism, both the traces within herself and the effects on black persons she knows intimately. Every white person who is struggling to throw off his or her racism should read it. And re-read it.

11. Michael Stocker, "Some Emotional Issues and Racism," paper read to conference, "Passions of the Color Line: Emotion and Power in Racial Construction," University of San Francisco, March 3, 2001.

12. Louis Althusser, "Ideology and Ideological State Apparatuses," in *Lenin and Philosophy and Other Essays*, trans. Ben Brewster (London: New Left Books, 1971).

13. See Charles Hoch, *What Planners Do: Power, Politics and Persuasion* (Chicago: Planners Press–American Planning Association, 1994).

14. See in particular Charles Herbert Stember, *Sexual Racism: The Emotional Barrier to an Integrated Society* (New York: Harper and Row, 1976); Calvin Hernton, *Sex and Racism* (New York: Doubleday and Co., 1965); Joel Kovel, *White Racism* (New York: Pantheon, 1970); W. J. Cash, *The Mind of the South* (New York: Vintage Books, 1941). For a highly sophisticated treatment of the origins of the desire to dominate, see Isaac Balbus, *Emotional Rescue, the Theory and Practice of a Feminist Father* (New York: Routledge, 1998).

15. Lazarre, *Beyond the Whiteness of Whiteness*, xvi.

16. Iris Young has pointed out the similarities between "common sense" used in this way Heidegger's concept of inauthenticity, of life lived in *das Man*, literally "the one" as in "One doesn't wear white shoes after Labor Day." So who is the one? Everyone and no one, no one in particular. The average everydayness of beliefs is taken over from "the one" without reflection on its origin or its truth. Young, "Residential Segregation and the Racial Contract," unpublished paper.

Index

~

About the Author

Sandra Lee Bartky is one of the towering figures of Second Wave feminist theory. The importance of her work, not only in feminist philosophy but also in the wider world of women's studies and feminist thought, cannot be exaggerated. She is an influential teacher, speaker, and activist and the author of *Femininity and Domination: Studies in the Phenomenology of Oppression*. She is professor of philosophy and gender and women's studies at the University of Illinois at Chicago.